The Last Days
of the
Longest War

The Last Days of the Longest War

9-11 Goes Back to Genesis

William M. Curtis, III

WINEPRESS **WP** PUBLISHING

Packaged by WinePress Publishing, PO Box 428, Enumclaw, WA 98022. The views expressed or implied in this work do not necessarily reflect those of WinePress Publishing. The author(s) is ultimately responsible for the design, content and editorial accuracy of this work.

Scripture: Where Scripture is quoted it is a literal translation by Dr. Curtis of the following texts:

Old Testament—Masoretic Text: *Biblia Hebraica*, 1973, Wuertemburg Bible Societies, Germany.

New Testament—Nestle-Aland Greek Text: *Novum Testamentum Graece*, 1971, United Bible Societies, London.

Where Scripture is merely referenced the reader may consult either The New King James or The New American Standard Bible, both of which are considered literal and accurate translations of the Hebrew and Greek original texts.

ISBN 1-57921-750-8
Library of Congress Catalog Card Number: 2004092978

Dedication

To Henry M. Morris: mentor, inspiration, and friend to thousands of scientists who hold the book of Genesis to be literal, historical, true, and scientifically accurate.

Contents

List of Illustrations

Preface

Last Days of the Longest War: 9–11 goes Back to Genesis,
takes the reader from the Creation through the Fall to
redemption and eternal glory. Dr. Bill Curtis has done us all a
favor with his exploration and explanation of history from eternity past to eternity future, and he has summarized it all in these
few pages!

As the Post-Christian West moves out of Secular Humanism
into Postmodernism with its ideas of "I have my truth and you
have your truth," moral relativism and evolutionary naturalism, a
reminder of the true truth of the Bible, especially the book of Genesis and of the Revelation is definitely in order. From coast to coast
in America, signs and bumper stickers say *God Bless America*, but
who is the God whose blessing we invoke since the horrors of 9–
11? Dr. Curtis clearly defines this one true God as the God of all
creation, the Almighty of the Bible.

According to the author, 9–11 is the defining event of our time.
The Trade Towers, the Pentagon, and Pennsylvania proved beyond
any doubt that a battle of worldviews is raging at the beginning of

the twenty-first century. But this battle is nothing new. It goes all the way back to the Garden of Eden about 6000 years ago. Here our ancestor Eve was deceived by Satan and ate of the forbidden fruit as did her willful husband, Adam, and the seed of 9–11 was planted. Down through the ages Satan has attempted to thwart almighty God's plan to redeem Adam's now-fallen race through the shedding of blood and death of God's only begotten Son, the Lord Jesus Christ.

With extensive presentation of modern scientific research, the case is made for a literal historical reading of the Genesis record. A six-day creation with its interdependence showing that nothing works until everything works, followed by a cursed Earth which fits the death and destruction we now experience, with a global flood as evidenced in the catastrophic geological evidence, and the dispersion of nations and continents, are all shown to fit the scientific studies. The cosmos is shown to fit a 6000-year time line not only biblically, but historically and scientifically as well.

Dr. Curtis ably defends his thesis that "9–11 is just the latest manifestation of the Long War Against God." That war began in Genesis 3:15 with God declaring to Satan: "And I will put enmity between thee and the woman, and between thy seed and her seed; He shall bruise thy head, and thou shall bruise his heel." This is the war that pervades our age and will not end until the devil and his seed are cast into the eternal lake of fire as described in the book of Revelation, chapter 20.

In between the beginning and the end, the Bible prophesied many things that are to come. *Last Days of the Longest War* documents many of these prophecies with particular emphasis on the battle through the ages between the descendants of Isaac and Ishmael. Dr. Curtis employs his vast knowledge of science to explain how technology is being utilized in the war against

God, and how the last hi-tech battles will be centered in and around Jerusalem. Christians and Jews are the target of the forces of evil in these last days, but this book makes it clear that the people of the one true God have always been targeted. As Jesus suffered (Hebrews 5:8), so will those who have put their faith and trust in Him (1 Peter 2:21).

An excellent case is made in this book from history, science, and prophecy that we are in the last moments of the end of this age. The coming of the Lord Jesus for His people could happen at any moment (1 Thessalonians 4:13–18). Dr. William Curtis' monograph should cause us all to examine ourselves to see if we are in the faith, and then to look up for our redemption draweth nigh!

—Dr. Jobe Martin, President
Biblical Discipleship Ministries, TX

Introduction

We who are trained by the Holy Scriptures in the knowledge of truth, do know both the beginning and the end of the world.
—Lactantius, Divine Institutes, c. A.D. 300

Man knows not his time.
—Cotton Mather, 1663–1728, Puritan
minister from a sermon

Richard Bernstein, writing for *The New York Times*, and commenting on Samuel Huntington's book, *The Clash of Civilizations and the Remaking of World Order*, stated that it was "A benchmark of informed speculation on those always fascinating questions: Just where are we in history? What hidden hand is controlling our destiny?" The Creator God of the Bible has given His creation the answers to these questions and this monograph should be seen as the definitive sequel to Huntington's book. This book is inspired by the understanding that apart from a truly biblical worldview, that is to say one based on a literal, historical interpretation of the book of Genesis, most people in the world today don't have a clue as to what time it is in our earthly sojourn or what is really going on in these last days of the current and climactic world scene. The author Ian McEwan wrote that "any story of beginning is an artifice, and what recommends one over another is how much sense it makes in what follows." This observation certainly applies to the Genesis record, and what this monograph will try to prove is that the world we know today and the recorded history of mankind, as well as the scientific knowledge of the past and present, certainly fit the Genesis account.

Before us now, brought to the forefront by the evil attack on the World Trade Center on 9-11-2001, the war in the Middle East and Israel, and the rise of all the players spoken of in the book of Revelation, are all the major components of the final conflict. This conflict began shortly after the dawn of creation when mankind, in the persons of Adam and Eve, disobeyed God and chose to follow Satan's lead. As a just result, God declared *war* between the *seed of Satan and God's chosen Seed of mankind* (Gen. 3:15). James Russell Lowell wrote a poem in the nineteenth century to address this ages-long struggle between good and evil that began in the Garden of Eden. Titled *Once to Every Man and Nation* it reads in part:

> Once to every man and nation
>   Comes the moment to decide,
> In the strife of truth with falsehood,
>   for the good or evil side . . .
> Then it is the brave man chooses,
>   While the coward stands aside,
> Til the multitude make virtue
>   Of the faith they had denied . . .
> Though the cause of evil prosper,
>   Yet 'tis truth alone is strong;
> Though her portion be the scaffold
>   And upon the throne be wrong,
> Yet that scaffold sways the future,
>   And, behind the dim unknown,
> Standeth God within the shadow,
>   Keeping watch above his own . . .

Introduction

Lowell described the struggle that began in the Garden of Eden, peaked at the cross of Calvary, and continues to this day. It is a battle between truth and falsehood, between good and evil, between freedom and slavery, between Christianity and all other religions, between light and darkness, between God and Satan. It has been *war*, going on for six thousand years, and will continue until the end of this age.

Comprehending this eternal, divinely mandated conflict is the key to understanding 9–11. This book, as it deals with the scriptural truths in Genesis, Job, Revelation etc., will lift the veil which blinds so many in our secular society, and help the reader, whether Christian believer or unbeliever, to understand this cosmic struggle and the Satanic operations behind the scene. This struggle and how to cope with it was clearly taught by the apostle Paul in the sixth chapter of his epistle to the Ephesians. We have now entered into what this author believes are *The Last Days of this Longest War*. To cope with the perils of the last days we must understand the true nature of the forces we confront today. The book of Genesis has always provided the foundation for understanding our world, our nature, and God's plan for His creation. It has been ignored or relegated to mythology, poetry, or symbolism or worse in much of today's world, both by scientists and churchmen, who through their ignorance, are too intimidated by the high priests of naturalism, and have disregarded the very foundation God gave us to understand His plan for mankind.

From Genesis to Revelation the Scriptures reveal a scenario of satanic enmity towards the believing seed. This enmity is the key to the cause for 9–11 and the entire world situation in these last days. This biblical worldview is the key to our understanding the perilous end times which are approaching. From the time of Charles Darwin's attack on the book of Genesis in the mid-nineteenth century, preceded by others such as Lyell and Hutton, who ignored the evidence for the Genesis flood and came up with the evolutionary geologic column just as the apostle Peter said they would in 2 Peter 3, our scientific and religious leaders have been feeding us a worldview with a distorted sense of history. With Genesis mythologized we have lost a biblical worldview regarding the conflict in the Middle East, the right of the Jews to a homeland in Jerusalem, the roots of anti-Semitism throughout the world, and the real reason we must confront Islam with the truth and with force. This monograph has integrated the latest creation science arguments with the Genesis record to show its veracity and applicability to the events of today's world.

The fundamental purpose of the Creation, and the true purposes of God in this temporal cosmos, can best be understood through the comparative analysis of God's revelation, man's scientific knowledge, and a thorough knowledge of world history. This understanding is truly comprehended with the integration of all three disciplines. With so many world events coming into focus in these last days, there is no better time to put the Scripture to the test to see what a truly God-breathed work it is.

The exegetical and scientific arguments for the literal, historical and scientific accuracy of the Genesis record are presented to the level that the average reader should be able to grasp the truth of these facts. Furthermore, an overview of the Holy Scripture is presented with both scientific and exegetical studies declaring its authenticity, accuracy, and authority. A brief synopsis of the entire panorama of history unfolds the past, the present, and the future in a scenario totally understandable in the confusion of the last days. This confusion has been exacerbated by the lies taught in the scientific and historical areas by secular education in our schools and media.

Introduction

The biblical presentation of God, His nature, and His purpose for the creation of mankind is simply stated and then we go behind the scenes to look at the creation of the heavenly hosts and the physical universe. God, Lucifer, Michael, in a scenario more interesting than Star Wars, will be presented. The rebellion in the heavenlies and the scene on Earth are examined as the existence of good and evil is explained.

As we study *the long war against God*, as Dr. Henry Morris has chosen to call this conflict, we will endeavor to bring everything into focus for this present time. This study of the history of mankind will necessarily be brief, but we will not attempt to rewrite history as has been in vogue with our secular educational system as well as every ungodly national entity in the past century from Hitler, to Stalin, to Arafat. This book will define the fundamental fault line which Samuel Huntington, in his aforementioned book titled *The Clash of Civilizations and the Remaking of World Order,* characterizes as the defining differences that will promulgate conflict in the twenty-first century. We will also look into the prophetic future, the nation of Israel, the Christian believers, the nation of Islam, and the world powers of the west, east, south and north as prophetically described. This monograph will provide understanding, hope, truth, and a plan of action for everyone who will read it.

Jesus said that if we do not believe Moses' writings, how shall we believe His words (John 5:46, 47). Likewise, it can be said that if we do not believe in a literal interpretation of the book of Genesis, we cannot understand: mankind's true condition, the existence of evil, the reason for death, the curse upon nature, the need for a savior, the nation of Israel, the history of the world and the purposes of God in it. Regarding our country's fight to retain the Ten Commandments in its public areas such as court buildings, state and national capitols, and public schools, it should

17

be known that Sir William Blackstone began his famous commentary on the laws of England by pointing out that Genesis was foundational to the very concepts of freedom and just law in a society. This treatise presents a Christian worldview based on transcendent truths as revealed to man in the Scriptures. So let us go back to Genesis and study *the long war against God*, biblically, historically, and scientifically.

CHAPTER 1

9–11 The Event that Defines Our Time

Men never do evil so completely and cheerfully as when they do it from religious conviction.

—Blaise Pascal, *Pensees*

When we think back on the events that have defined our time many of us can remember Pearl Harbor, or VJ Day (the day that WW II ended with Japan's surrender), or the day that President Kennedy was assassinated. So it will be for this current generation, that September 11, 2001 (9–11) will be that day. We remember where we were, and when, and how we heard. So let me reminisce a bit as we set the scene that will define our immediate future and the need for this monograph.

It was the morning of September 11 2001. We were concluding the last sessions on the last day of The Friends of Israel[1] prophecy conference at Willow Valley conference center in Lancaster, PA. The featured guest speaker, a Jewish gentleman, had just declared that the leaders of Islam have sworn to "get rid of the Saturday people and then they were going after the Sunday people." Upon hearing of the attack in New York, the entire conference emptied to go out into the hallway to watch on television the horrific sights occurring at the World Trade Center, at the Pentagon, and in a small field in Pennsylvania.

The conference immediately went to prayer and followed this time with some final thoughts from the various speakers. Having long understood the antipathy that Islam has for the world of Christians and particularly the Jews, it is of little surprise that the more fanatical elements would attack the centers of Christian world power. The attacks were slated to destroy the foremost symbol of our economic power, and our governmental centers. While a major blow was achieved with the destruction of the World Trade Center, and a portion of The Pentagon, it was through divine providence and the efforts of several brave souls on flight 93 that the White House or the Capitol was spared.

The Islamic war against Christians and Jews goes back some 1400 years. The lust of Muslim imperialists has been against hundreds of nations, over millions of square miles. The terror and wars ranged from the lands of the Middle East through the times of the Crusades, to the lands of southern France, to the Pacific, and from Austria to Africa. The classic definition of imperialism is "the policy and practice of seeking to dominate the economic and political affairs of other countries." With its Arabic base, the object was always submission to Muslim control with Christians and Jews and anyone else having to submit to Koranic authority. There is no freedom or tolerance in this system. Today this system has declared subjection of the whole world as its ultimate objective which will be documented in following chapters.

I am not sure where our news media has been with respect to Islam these last twenty years or even since the turn of the previous century, but probably the kindest statement could be "out to lunch." Consider that Islam massacred 1.5 million Armenians in the first part of the twentieth century with hardly any Western news media acknowledgment. Armenia was considered to be the first nation, in the third Christian century, to embrace Christianity on a national scale. The part that Islam played in this genocide is largely overlooked and today the obfuscation goes on. Muslim Libya has blown up aircraft and financed northern Sudan. Muslim northern Sudan has conquered much of southern Sudan, enslaving and murdering more than a million people, many of whom are Christians. Indonesia's Muslim rulers have sought to subjugate the people of New Guinea, East Timor, and the Celebes with horrible loss of life. Muslim Albania (called ethnic Albania by our ignorant press) is still attempting to press its advantage against the Serbs and Croatia. Muslim northern Nigeria will murder Nigerian Christians at the slightest excuse. A half-dozen Arab countries have fought four wars in an attempt to destroy Israel with the publicly voted consent of fifty-five of the world's fifty-seven Islamic nations. And last but not least is Iraq, which has waged wars resulting in death to some two million people in the past twenty years and exists as a threat to Christians and Jews wherever they can reach them.

As this book goes to press the war in Iraq (ancient Babylon) continues. This war, which brings us back to the sands that gave rise to the world's earliest civilizations, has been called *The War that will Change the World* by Ralph Peters, writing for *The New York Post* (March 20, 2003). This war, which was triggered by the events of 9–11 and Islam's long enmity against Israel and the USA, will change the face of the Middle East till the last days of this age. Just as Teddy Roosevelt shattered the influence of the old world empires in the Western hemisphere with the short Spanish American War and set us on the century-long road to defeat of the old world powers of kings, emperors, dictators, and czars (Caesars), so will the war in Iraq set the tone for the epochal war with Islamic tyranny in the rest of the world. It should be obvious that this war will not defeat the evil empire of Satan which dwells in many nations. But it is true that this war will change the world, as Satan is in the final throes of his worldwide war against the family of God.

It is the thesis of this monograph that this war did not begin with Islam in the seventh century A.D., nor with any of the other Satan-inspired attacks on the Creator and His children who lie in Adam, but began in the garden of Eden where God declared *war* between the *Seed of the woman and the seed of Satan* (Gen. 3:15). It should be understood that 9–11 is not terrorism but is *religious war!*

Thousands of people died in the World Trade Center, but millions of people die every day, because all humans have been given the death penalty as recorded in Genesis chapter three. Why did God allow 9–11? The answer is woven throughout the Scripture, and Jesus dealt with it in His discussion about the tower of Siloam falling as recorded in Luke's gospel chapter thirteen. We are in a *war*, and I believe this war is in its *last days,* so we say that 9–11 defines our times, and we indeed can look forward to the consummation of this *long war against God*, which has been brought to a worldwide scale. It is hoped this book will establish the book of Genesis as the foundation for all our thinking in the minds of everyone who reads this.

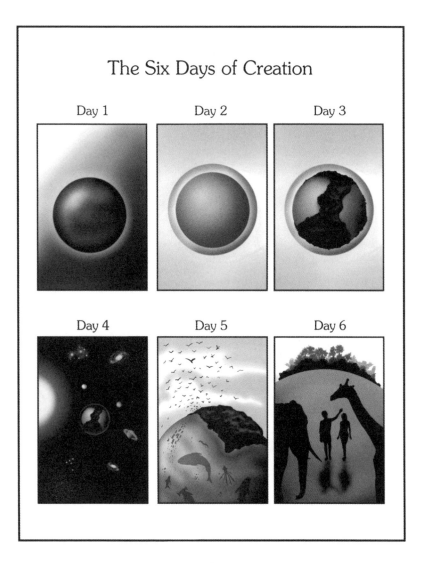

The Six Days of Creation

Day 1	Day 2	Day 3
Day 4	Day 5	Day 6

6 Days of Creation

CHAPTER 2

Genesis: Literal, Historical, Foundational Truth

For if you believed Moses, you would believe Me; for he wrote about me. But if you do not believe his writings, how will you believe My words?

—Jesus, John 5:46–47

The remainder of the Bible stands or falls on the Genesis record. Dr. Henry Morris has said, "The book of Genesis is probably the most important book ever written."[2] It also might be rightly said that an understanding of the entire cosmos, i.e. world, is only perceived from a literal, historical understanding of Genesis. So, we begin with Genesis and bring the reader down through history to the present and then move into the prophetic future with a monograph of precious truth in these last days.

A. Genesis Creation—6 Days Exegetically

The New Testament gives us a mandate for interpreting Genesis. In every New Testament reference to Genesis the events and people are treated as true, literal, historical accounts. The first chapter of the book of Genesis clearly states that the entire universe was created by God in six days. Both the Scripture and the scientific evidence are strongly on the side of this literal reading of Genesis. No honest student of Hebrew should deny that the writers of Genesis *intended* to convey that God created the heavens and the earth in six literal days, just as we experience today. This is a truth which the Jews declare to this day by their observance of the Sabbath which was to be a sign forever of the six days of creation: "Wherefore the children of Israel shall keep the Sabbath, to observe the Sabbath throughout their generations, a perpetual covenant. It is a sign between me and the children of Israel forever; for in six days the LORD made heaven and earth, and on the seventh day he rested, and was refreshed" (Ex. 31:16–17, 20:11).

The Hebrew word *Yom,* translated as *day* in English, always means a twenty-four hour period including darkness and light when *Yom* is preceded by an ordinal number, and evening and morning are in the context. This is exactly the way it is used in all six days of creation in Genesis chapter one (Gen. 1:5, 8, 13, 19, 23, 31).

Furthermore, it is certain that Jesus held that the creation account and all of Genesis was a literal, historical document with His references to Adam and Eve in marriage (Matt. 19, Mark 10:6–8), the Sabbath (Mark 2:27, Luke 6:5), and Noah's days (Matt. 24:38, 39, Luke 17:27). The apostle Paul clearly refers to Adam's fall as the reason we all die (Rom. 5:12). There are over 165 passages in Genesis directly quoted or referred to in the New Testament; nowhere is there the slightest evidence that these passages were myths or allegories. All men know in their hearts the implication of the Creator/creation relationship (Rom. 1:18–32; 9:17–23). I was once asked by an evolutionist if one had to believe in the Genesis record of creation to be a believer in Christ. The book of Hebrews answers this very question. Hebrews 11:3 makes belief in creation by divine fiat the very essence of faith itself: "By faith we understand that the worlds were framed by the word of God, so that the things which are seen were not made of things which are visible." Creation out of nothing by a transcendent Creator called *Elohim* is fundamental to belief in Him, as is salvation from a condemned and warring world (John 3:16–18). Genesis must be presented as rational, historic truth if the rest of the Bible is to be believed. Truth in science certainly will back up this position as the following will show.

B. Genesis Creation—6 Days Scientifically

There are many discoveries in the current state of the art in biological science, astronomy, nuclear physics, genetic research, DNA, and information theory, as well as several other scientific disciplines such as archaeology and sedimentology which are consistent with the Genesis record of not only six, twenty-four hour days of creation, but a young earth as never before understood.

The many symbiotic relationships between flora and fauna, [i.e. both dependent on each other for life, and both present at the same time], demand their coexistence at the start. An example is the fact that much of the vegetation (flora) in existence requires pollination by bird and insect species (fauna) which must be alive and present for the vegetation to survive. The facetious statement by evolutionists that the wind could have provided this pollination is proven wrong by many instances where only a particular bird or insect can pollinate certain flora.

This interdependency, i.e. everything needs to all be working at once, is also true of the physical relationship of the sun, moon, and the earth. The balance in the present positions of these heavenly bodies is absolutely essential to the sustenance of life on earth. Not only can it be said that we are living on a knife edge, but we know from scientific studies that these relationships are changing:

the sun is shrinking/burning up and the moon is changing its orbit, all of which fit only a young solar system scenario. These changes also fit the Second Law of Thermodynamics, which states that everything is progressing from order to disorder. This law, which has been tested repeatedly, fits every test of a scientific law, and a creation model—good in the beginning and falling away with every passing moment.

The chemical elements of the universe, which modern science has discovered here on Earth, and observed from the spectrographic study of light from distant galaxies, stars etc., and confirmed with trips to the moon, Mars, and even asteroids, are the same throughout the universe, complete in their makeup, and are not evolving. The late Sir Fred Hoyle, one of the leading nuclear physicists of this past century, in his early days, wrote an evolutionary treatise on creating the elements in space.[3] But the more Hoyle studied their ordered nature and their obviously limited number, the more he realized that they were not evolving. In a later effort by these two scientists titled, *Where Microbes Boldly Went,*[4] it was stated that the probability that biochemical evolution could occur by chance was determined to be less than one in ten to the forty-thousandth power. In Hoyle's last years he became an advocate for creation prior to his entering into God's presence in 2003.

Regarding, first of all, the stable elements, they are all complete from number one (hydrogen) to number 92 (uranium), with no missing elements. With regard to the highly unstable radioactive elements above uranium, all of which are created in laboratories, it should be understood that these are not basic elements of the created universe, but merely matter and energy transformations related to Einstein's $E=mc2$ which are transient and fit the first and second laws of thermodynamics (1. No energy or matter can be created or destroyed, 2. Everything is progressing from order to disorder). Each artificially created element above uranium has a shorter and shorter life determined mathematically by the relation of binding energy to atomic mass number which prohibits the evolution of elements and predicts the decrease of half life with each succeeding atomic number. For example, the half life of Einsteinium, atomic number 99, is one year, and the half life of nobelium, atomic number 102, is 60 minutes, and atomic number 109 is .005 seconds. As recently as February 1, 2004 it was reported in *Physical Review C*, a leading chemistry journal, that the elements of atomic number 115 and 113 were synthesized by a team of Russian and American scientists. What was not said in the article was that these elements fit the ever-decreasing half-life predictions, and were, I am sure, a great disappointment to the evolutionary scientists who predicted and hoped that 113 would be a stability plane and 115 would show that it is possible for elements to evolve to a higher order. In conclusion, the elements, which are the same everywhere in the known universe, are complete in their stable form and are not evolving, nor can they, as we have proven in the nuclear physics research of this past century!

Regarding the great distances in space and the apparent time required for light to reach us from these distant galaxies, recent work by Dr. Humphreys, Ph.D. in physics, has offered a scientifically sound solution to our young earth and the Genesis record. This solution involves Einstein's general theory of relativity and the gravitational time dilation in the universe. Dr. Humphreys has published several papers on this relationship and one book titled *Starlight and Time* (Master Books, Colorado Springs CO, 1995). Furthermore, evolutionary cosmology is in serious trouble with regard to the Big Bang theory. The Big Bang certainly cannot and does not answer the causality question of why anything exists, or who or what caused it in the first place. The Big Bang and the expanding universe theory is so seriously flawed scientifically that several renowned astronomers and physicists have pronounced it dead! (see books by Halton Arp, David Berlinski, Wendell Bird, William Corliss, Don DeYoung, Fred Hoyle, and Jayant Narliker, just to name a few). There are at least five fundamental scientific principles that it violates: 1. The conservation of angular momentum. 2. The first and second laws of thermodynamics. 3. The cosmic background radiation is not homogeneous and isotropic as it should be if it had been produced by an explosion from a central source. 4. The universe is not uniform in large-scale structure, as both Big Bang and Steady State theories require. This lumpy universe, with large agglomerations of matter in some places and vast empty spaces in others, defies any natural formation mechanism. 5. An explosion cannot be shown to draw matter together; the amount of matter required to draw the known matter together by gravitational forces is not detectable by any means. This caused the noted physicist Stephen Hawking to say that ninety-five percent of the universe is in "cold/dark matter" and has led to the speculative nonsense of massive black holes which of course we cannot see since by definition no light can escape from a mass so dense.

There is a need of even the simplest living cells for basic DNA instructions, i.e. information from outside, which Plato referred to as *The Logos*, "the divine thought behind the existence of everything." Dr. Werner Gitt from Germany's Federal Institute of Physics and Technology in Braunschweig, explains in his information theory studies that there must be information from outside the inanimate entity for it to change into an animate entity. Dr. Gitt has challenged the evolutionist with the statement that, "There is no known natural law through which matter can give rise to information, neither is any physical process or material phenomenon known that can do this." This statement has remained unanswered since it was first published over a decade ago.

Furthermore, it is clear that these cells which need DNA information cannot change incrementally by chance without this basic information, nor can they survive in any intermediate condition. Dr. Michael Behe in his book *Darwin's Black Box* has conclusively shown that even the simplest living cell cannot have incremental changes in its DNA or any of its other mechanisms and survive. They are "irreducibly complex." In short, the creation must be caused by something outside itself with information from an all-knowing source, as the increasingly developed intelligent design movement is showing. It must be understood that the universe with life here on Earth had to be complete in six days because *nothing works until everything works!*

Of further interest is the fact that mitochondrial DNA (mtDNA) is replicated in the woman, and all living Homo sapiens have this identical mtDNA. This fact, when first discovered in the mid-1980s, caused the press to start referring to Mother Eve. Evolutionary geneticists who realized they had just given the creationist the greatest scientific evidence for the Genesis record (that all humans descended from one woman) that anyone could imagine, have spent the last two decades trying to explain it away with bogus data. An example of this was in a University of Utah article, *Learning to Tell Time* by P. Sahm; *Health Sciences Report*, Summer 2002, pp. 12–15. What is truly humorous about these studies is their firm statement that "modern humans arose in Africa 100,000–200,000 years ago" (p. 14). This is based on the fact their data shows that the human population and the mtDNA variation is just too small to support millions of years. These data will eventually come back to haunt them as their own dates of 200,000 years disagrees with the Leakey, Johansen, *National Geographic* dates for Lucy et al. of 4.5 million years. The 4.5 million number is based on what strata of rock the fossils were found in, and dated by the bogus geological column of evolutionary theory. Significant research in the past 20 years at the

Grand Canyon, Mt. St. Helens, The State University of Colorado and Sedimentology labs in France have shown that the geological column is a product of the world wide catastrophic flood that covered the whole earth. These data are now being allowed to be presented at the Grand Canyon National Park museum.

C. Genesis—Foundation of History

Genesis gives us the *what* and *why* for all of the foundationally important aspects necessary to understand this world system (Greek: *cosmos*). The following examples are given:

1. Origin of the universe by a supreme transcendent eternal being who is called God in the English language, and in the Hebrew, *Elohim*. This universe includes all measurable matter and energy. Thus, we understand a space-mass-time continuum, which is created and not eternal as all other cosmologies assert. The first days speak of the heavens as plural, which comprise the entire universe other than the earth. The earth is a separate entity, which is created out of nothing and bathed in light by God. It should be seen that the physical elements are all created and energized by God, but the transformation of the earth, which is said to be without form and void (Gen. 1:2), goes on throughout the six days as first it is raised out of the water on the second day (Gen. 1:9), endued with flora on the third day, lit with the heavenly stars, planets, galaxies etc. on the fourth day, populated with sea and airborne creatures on the fifth day, and finally with the land creatures and man on the sixth day.

2. Origin and purpose for the stars, sun, moon, and planets, which are created for man's edification (Gen. 1:14;

Isa. 40:26) and direction. These heavenly bodies were created subsequent to the creation of light, which emanates from God Himself.

3. Origin of the dry land called earth, with land fit for habitation by man.

4. Origin of life with its myriad of complexities, which defy any other explanation than creation by an infinite Creator. The biological scientist J. B. S. Haldane said, "Not only is the world queerer than you imagine, it is queerer than you can imagine." Life is truly too complex to have evolved without a divine thought (Greek: *Logos*) behind the information required to make the DNA work.

5. Origin of sex, man and woman, and marriage. The need for a perfectly compatible biological mate is a process which is totally against the Darwinian evolutionary theory of survival of the fittest. The sexual union of two perfectly matched beings required to propagate has long been recognized as an evolutionary impossibility. Man, created in the image of God, unique among all living beings with a mate required, will be dealt with in depth in chapter 3.

6. Fixity of kinds, which is evidenced in the fossil record and the living record. This truth is so evident, even to some evolutionists, that there are arguments between Darwinian evolutionists, who speak of small incremental variations over great periods of time, and punctuated equalibria evolutionists such as the late Stephen Jay Gould who admitted that there is no evidence of transitional forms in the living or fossil record, so it must have happened instantaneously at different times, one step at a time.

7. Origin of evil and death as testified to by every living being, which will be dealt with at length in chapter 4.

8. Origin of the nation of Israel and the nations that oppose her. Chapter 6 will bring this into focus regarding the present conflict.

9. A time line, which can be traced from the present, back to the creation of this present earth, mankind, and all that exists within our present ability to see.

Beyond these fundamental origins, Genesis will help us to understand the present conflicts with regard to the children of God and the children of the devil, which gives us true insight into 9–11, anti-Semitism, and a whole host of ancillary issues. Furthermore, the entire body of Holy Scripture is to be understood as supernatural revelation from the Creator and as such should be considered as authoritative and the standard of truth. Consider following proofs of this statement: The entire body of the Old Testament, the Hebrew Scriptures, was said by Jesus to prophesy of Him (Matt. 5:17). For 2000 years the Hebrew prophets wrote, and in over 300 statements, Christ was the fulfillment of these prophecies. Matthew cites twenty-seven specific texts that Christ directly fulfilled at His first coming. The mathematical probability that the Messiah was or could be in the future anyone other than Jesus is essentially zero. Just to cite a biblical text that shows how future events are considered to be mathematically probable that they were given by an all-knowing God we cite 1 Samuel 10:2–6 which gave a series of prophetic statements to Elijah of events that were to shortly happen in sequence which were perfectly fulfilled. The probability that this statement was not from an omniscient Creator is less than one in twenty-one factorial. This number, as most know, is 21 x 20 x 19 x 18 etc. on down to 1, which is a number that exceeds the number of stars estimated in the cosmos or even the late Carl Sagan's favorite statement of "billions of billions."

There are over 2,000 specific prophecies in the Bible which have already been fulfilled. There are no such prophecies in the scriptures of any other religion. The writings of Buddha are totally bereft of any sort of predicted events on the future. In the writings of Confucius there are no predictive prophecies. In the Koran, the scriptures of Islam, we find only the prophecy of Mohammed that he would return to Mecca, which he himself fulfilled. In the writings of Joseph Smith, the Mormon prophet, there were several prophecies which *did not* come true as prophesied! Only in the Holy Scriptures called the Bible have there been so many specific, concrete, and exact fulfillments. Thus, we should be able to trust them when they speak of the "last days."

It is with this understanding of the unique nature of the Holy Scripture and the extensive archaeological work over the past century that has verified most of the biblical record beyond what the liberal scholars could imagine that we enter into the next chapter of purely biblical studies of the fundamental purpose of God's creation of the cosmos and man.

God Creates Man

CHAPTER 3

Genesis: God and His Purposes for Man

You are worthy, O Lord to receive glory and honor and power; for You created all things, and by Your will they exist and were created.
—Revelation 4:11

A. God

The universe, with its intelligent design and bewildering complexity from the infinitesimal to the vastness of space, bears the stamp of an infinite creator. It is the stamp of purpose! The universe is not an accident, nor an evolutionary development. We are said to be able to discern these truths (Rom. 1:19–20). Furthermore, God revealed His purpose through His inspiration of His prophets in the Holy Scriptures.

The Scriptures state that God created the heavens, the earth, and all that is in them (Gen. 1:1–16; Ex. 20:11, 31:16–17; John 1:1–3; Col. 1:12–20). In defining God, we look to His person, His attributes, His works, and His purposes. Having established Genesis as truth from exegetical, historical, and scientific studies in the previous chapter, we can now delve into the nature of this

Creator and His purposes. This brief overview is not intended to be exhaustive, but it is hoped sufficient to understand the creation and the present *long war against God.*

His Person

As a transcendent, almighty Creator God, His very attributes demand a complex, eternal, infinite being, manifested in three persons as He is revealed in Scripture as Father, Son and Holy Spirit (Matt. 28:19–20; Col. 1:12–20). God's unity is further revealed as the Son was also called Eternal Father, Almighty God, and Prince of Peace (Isa. 9:6). The Scripture declares that God has been revealed in these latter days "in the Son" (Heb. 1:1–3). He and His Son called themselves "the self-existing one," the great I AM (Ex. 3:14; John 8:24, 58). As Father, He is the thought and information behind all that exists, which was Plato's definition of the *Logos* (John 1:1). The Father is said to be light (1 John 1:5) into which we cannot look (1 Tim. 6:16). The Son thus is a unique manifestation of God given to man that we might understand this transcendent One (John 1:14, 10:30, 14:10; 1 Tim. 6:11–15). The Son is a member of the eternal triune Godhead (Col. 1:13–20, 2:9) who existed in eternity before the world was (John 17:5). The Son was sent as the seed of a woman to reveal a loving Creator God to His creation, and provide a solution to man's fallen condition (John 3:16). Thus, a just and righteous creator is also shown to be a loving God (1 John 4:8).

Explaining the Holy Spirit is a whole study in itself which is not the purpose of this monograph; suffice it to say that the Spirit is the third person of the Godhead (Matt. 28:19; John 4:24), who is sent to us by the Father and the Son (John 16:7–15). This Spirit today dwells within the true children of God as all who have received Him know (Rom. 8:14–17).

His Attributes

Holy is the word used to express a perfection that is totally other, separate. This is the true Hebrew meaning of the word. So God is to be seen as separate from man and His creation. Only God is Holy in this sense (Ps. 145:17; Isa. 6:3; Rev. 4:8). God is righteous (Rom. 3:10; 1 John 2:1), just (Rom. 3:26; 1 John 1:9) omnipotent (Gen. 1), omniscient (Ps. 33:13, 90:8; Isa. 46:10; Acts 15:18; Rom. 4:17; Heb. 4:13), omnipresent (Ps. 139), and last of all, loving (1 John 4:7–10).

His Works

His primary works of Creation, revelation, and redemption through His Son, are all recorded for us throughout the Scripture, from Genesis to Revelation. God has worked throughout history, and continues to work in the world that He created. These efforts are all recorded for mankind in the biblical and secular record if we could just remove the satanic veil from men's eyes.

His Purposes for Mankind

It is God's will that there will be an eternal kingdom that will be governed by Him, where we will live and reign with Him. This is perfectly explained in the prayer Jesus taught His disciples, erroneously called *The Lord's Prayer*: Our Father which art in heaven (His children); Thy kingdom come, Thy will be done (His kingdom, His will); on earth as in heaven (place and time yet future for Earth)—Matt. 6:9–13; Lk. 11: 2–4. This is further prophesied in the scenes on Earth and in heaven (Rev. 4:11; 20–22). The created universe was initially a picture of a theocratic kingdom where mankind would live, exercising royal domain over the earth (Gen. 1:28), as God's representative in a peaceful and filial relationship. In ancient Near East texts, only the king was considered to be unto the very image of God, a relationship that still existed in the minds of the Romans in the days of the Caesars. This very reason is why Pilate was so worried when he heard of Christ's claim to be the Son of God (Jn. 19: 7–9). Thus, mankind was created by God to be His children (Rom. 8:16–17), created in His image (Gen. 1:26–27), with free will to choose, and as such we were to glorify the Father, have fellowship with the Father, and live and reign with Him forever (Matt. 6:9–15; Lk. 11:2–4; Rev. 20–22).

The temporal creation of Earth was to provide a testing ground, i.e. a dispensation in time, in which mankind would be given the freedom to choose the kingdom of God or to choose the kingdom of Satan. The heavenly kingdom is to be an "everlasting kingdom of our Lord and Savior Jesus Christ" (2 Pet. 1:11). All those who are called out of this world, from Abel to Abraham, to the vast numbers amongst the Gentiles (Acts 15:14) will in these last days be involved in this mighty struggle for the souls of men. The fundamental purpose of the cosmos in our present situation must be understood in this light.

B. Man

Mankind, in the persons of Adam and Eve, was created in God's image (Gen. 1–2), and able to share in the procreative process of bringing children into the world. Angels were not made in God's image or able to create other angels. They were created to serve God and man, but with their own free will. The origin of the existence of the physical and moral evils in the universe is explained in Scripture as a temporary intrusion into God's perfect creation, allowed by Him, as a concession to the principle of *freedom* and responsibility. C. S. Lewis said that "God created things which had free will—and free will, though it makes evil possible, is also the only thing that makes possible any love or joy worth having."[5] The free will defense has been well understood to exonerate God from the charge of incapacity to prevent events such as 9–11. Thus, an omnipotent Creator, having created free beings, must leave what transpires partly up to them.

God thus manifests Himself as an omnipotent Creator, perfect in every attribute, holy, righteous and just, and thus, created man was able to choose between good and evil. Furthermore, God, knowing that man would choose to know both good and evil and cause the whole creation to fall under the curse which evil brings, provided a way that He could manifest Himself as a perfect loving creator. This way was to enter into mankind in the person of His Son and give Himself to death and become the redeemer who paid the price for our redemption (Eph. 1:7; Col. 1:14; 1 Pet. 1:18). It is thus through the cross that God unites His attributes of righteousness and love. God wills love, love requires choice, and choice allows evil.

Man is said to be a trichotomous being, consisting of a body, a living soul, and spirit (Gen. 2:7). No other being created in days three through six has the spirit of God (spirit, and breath are the same Hebrew word *ruach*) giving it life, and is said to be created in the image of the Creator. It is through this spirit/mind that we have been given language so we can communicate in both the real and the abstract. No animal, despite years of research, has been taught to speak and reason in the abstract. We have a language we can speak and communicate with God and fellow man, and a mind with which we have a realization of eternity, love, justice, holiness, and the future, just as God has revealed it to us. Man is given the godly ability to be procreative, which is not given to angelic beings. God has not only declared that man was created in His image, but that the entire material universe was created for God's purpose for man. This is called the anthropic principle, which aggravates Satan and his followers to no end.

Satan, the Shining One, Speaking to Adam and Eve

CHAPTER 4

The Long War Against God Begins

I have read a fiery gospel writ in burnish'd rows of steel, As ye deal with my contemmers, So with you my grace shall deal; Let the Hero, born of woman, crush the serpent with his heel, Since God is marching on.

—The Battle Hymn of the Republic; verse sung at 9–11 memorial service at the National Cathedral just following 9–11.

As we approach the Genesis record on how *the Long War against God* began, it is interesting that President Bush chose the verse from the Battle Hymn that dealt with Genesis 3:15 and *the Long War against God*. It will be seen that at least one of our past presidents (see quote at the start of chapter 8) and I believe our current President Bush, understand what is behind the world crisis, and what to expect in the future and end of the age. So let us begin "In the beginning" (Gen. 1:1).

A. Satan and the Existence of Evil

There is no more enigmatic being in all of creation than the one who is called Satan. The Scripture presents him as the personal supreme spirit of evil, the tempter, and spiritual enemy of mankind. This *evil one* is the adversary of God although subordinate to Him and able to act only by His sufferance (Job 1:6–12). Lucifer was said to be first among the angels with great beauty and splendor (Ezek. 28:11–17). That Satan and the other angels were created before man is clearly indicated by God as He speaks to Job (Job 38:7). But there was iniquity possible in these other created beings and Satan (Hebrew), or in the Greek *diabolos* i.e. devil, became the first sinner. Satan is proud (Ezek. 28:17), ambitious (Isa. 14:12–17), and jealous of man. It should be pointed out that these passages in Ezekiel and Isaiah are actually identifying the rulers of Babylon and Tyre with Satan, for it is Satan who motivates these rulers with the same pride and belief that were true of him when he rebelled against God. Therefore, the rulers of this world who are evil, in whom Satan has reproduced his own wicked bent, have become virtual shadows of him and as such become the *seed* of Satan who are at war with the godly *seed* of the woman who are the children of God. This is the fault line war which was announced in Genesis 3:15, as will be explained in depth in the following section, which has brought us to 9–11. This fault line war, where we saw the face and felt the hand of evil, will be traced down through history in chapter 6.

With regard to man Satan is a seducer (Gen. 3), a liar (Gen. 3 and many New Testament passages such as Jn. 8). He seeks to devour man for his own kingdom of darkness (1 Pet. 5:8). He is called the god of this age (2 Cor. 4:3), who takes away the seed sown by God in His Word from those who are not pure in heart (Mk. 4:14–20). Satan is also called the prince of demons (Matt.

9:34, 12:24) and the prince of the power of the air (Eph. 2:2). Satan was seen as "a great red dragon" who sought to devour the Christ child as soon as He was born (Rev. 12:1–5). Satan can take on the appearance of an angel of light as Lucifer and is able to deceive many even in this age (2 Cor. 11: 14). At this time Satan and his agents have been cast down to roam the earth causing events like 9–11 (Eph. 6:10–17; 2 Tim. 2:24; 1 Pet. 5:8). God will continue to allow Satan to be loose for now, at least until the time spoken of in Revelation chapter 20, while He completes the forming of His kingdom family, so we should not be surprised by events like 9–11 occurring. There has been continuous warfare between the seed of the serpent, i.e. Satan, and the seed of the woman from the time of Genesis 3:15 until the last days of this present age.

Rebellion and war in heaven (Isa. 14:12–17; Ezek. 28:11–19; Rev. 12) is pictured in these passages. Satan's final abode is fixed in the lake of fire (Isa. 24:21; Matt. 25:41; Rev. 20: 1–3, 7, 10). Chapter 10 will spend some effort on how to deal with Satan in this present age.

What caused Satan to rebel and the many angels to follow him? Could it have been God's creation of man who was created in God's image (Gen. 2), to be judge of Satan's fallen gang of angels. The apostle Paul points out in his letter to the church at Corinth that we will judge angels (1 Cor. 6:3). Man, under Christ, will be the ruler of the coming theocratic kingdom (Rev. 20; Matt. 25) and ruler over the angels as Hebrews 2:5 states: "For He has not put the world to come, of which we speak, in subjection to angels," i.e., mankind will rule the world to come with Christ. It should be noted that in the eternal state, man will be as the angels and no longer in the creation mode as man and wife, i.e. no marriage, and of course no death (Mk. 12:25–27; Lk. 20:34–36).

It appears evident that Satan, as did all the other angels, observed the creation of man (Job 38:7). But Satan did not accept that he too was created, and as he was present at the creation of man, as was God so he could imagine that he was eternal or that he evolved as God must have too. Hence, it was a short step to want to be as God, just as he tempts mankind (Gen. 3: 3–5), and that Satan, hoping to exalt himself to godhood, would be the proponent of evolution from that day to this. Thus, Satan tempts mankind with the promise that we can be as gods, which is also the promise of Mormonism. See Joseph Smith's *King Follet* sermon, or Bruce McConkie's *Mormon Doctrine.*[6] It is very interesting the way both the Mormons and the Theosophical Society view the fall of man. In volume two of *The Secret Doctrine*, Madame Blavatsky wrote: "It is natural to view Satan, the Serpent of Genesis, as the real creator and benefactor, the Father of Spiritual mankind. For it is he who was the 'Harbinger of Light,' bright radiant Lucifer, who opened the eyes of the automaton created by Jehovah, as alleged; and he who was the first to whisper: 'in the day ye eat thereof ye shall be as Elohim, knowing good and evil.'"

Beyond this understanding of the author of evil, there needs to be an understanding of the results of the fall of mankind and the judgment of this world with Satan's continuing fight for preeminence. The Scripture notes that the rain falls on the just and the unjust (Matt. 5:45); Jesus later points out that many were killed when the Tower of Siloam fell (Lk. 13:4), and makes the point that these were not judged as greater or lesser sinners, but all mankind will perish unless we are redeemed. This begs the question regarding earthquakes, tornadoes, and airplanes crashing (i.e. 9–11) etc. How can we respond? Chapter 10 will deal with this in depth, but suffice it to say that we can pray for protection from this evil system as Jesus taught us to, and we can turn to God for this power and redemption before it is too late. We cannot claim we have the power for health and wealth until this age is over as Hebrews 11:36–39 clearly shows. The Scripture clearly points out that in this age we are subject to persecution (1 Pet.), and death, as we all lie in Adam (Rom. 5:12). There is eternal life available to all those whom God gives the ability to choose His solution in Christ. To those who are infants and incompetent, i.e. unable to choose, God has earned the right to redeem them through the completed work of His Son. Let it be said again that this is not the best world, but that our Creator has decided that it is the best path to the best world. The Scripture declares that Christ, through His death, has destroyed this devil who had the power of death (Heb. 2:14; 1 Jn. 3:8) and thus we see the way to the best world, i.e. the new heaven and new earth in the consummate age to come as will be explained in chapter 9.

B. Deception and the Fall of Man

Dominion over the Earth, which had been given to man (Gen. 1:28–30), was handed over to Satan by Adam and Eve, so a righteous God passed judgment on man and the earth (Gen. 3). Death came to the living beings, the environment was cursed, Satan was told where he stood, and the *proto-evangelium*, which is really a proto declaration of war, is all recorded in Genesis 3. It is not known how soon after the sixth day of creation that this temptation occurred, but it was probably in the next week as Adam and Eve were eating and observing the animals. It was certainly before Eve conceived her first child Cain (Gen. 4:1). Satan, first of all, lied to Adam and Eve telling them that the sin of disobedience would not cause death as God had said (Gen. 3:3–5). Satan promised what he could not deliver when he told mankind that we would be as God (verse 4). God wrote the battle plan out for Satan when He said to him, "I will put hatred (enmity/war) between thee and the woman, and between thy *seed* and her *seed; he shall crush thy head, and thou shalt bruise his heel* (Gen. 3:15). The seed of the woman has been generally acknowledged throughout Scripture and history as the godly seed and eventually as God's seed in Christ (a case which the apostle Paul makes specifically in Galatians 3:16), and is the hero in *The Battle Hymn of the Republic.* On the other hand the satanic seed with all of its ramifications in mankind, such as Cain, Nimrod, Mohammed, Hitler, Stalin, Saddam Hussein etc., has often been overlooked as a few evil people, or some unbelieving scientists, evolutionists, etc., or some other religion of which we must be tolerant. It should be clearly understood that Satan's seed consists of all unsaved people (1 Jn. 3:10), and the seed of the woman consists of the "remnant of her seed, which keep the commandments of God, and have the testimony of Jesus Christ" (Rev. 12:17)! Thus *the long war against God*, between the two seeds, has raged throughout history, and 9–11 is to be understood as a religious event promulgated by Satan's seed.

Thus, we see the battle of Satan's seed with the seed of the woman as explicitly stated in Revelation 12:17 as a war between the dragon and the seed of the woman who keep the commandments of God and have the testimony of Jesus Christ. This war has raged from the time of the fall in the Garden of Eden until this present time as man abides under the curse (Gen. 3) and will abide under the curse of death until it is removed in the new heaven and earth (Rev. 21, 22). Since death is pronounced upon all mankind during this time (Heb. 9:27), Satan will wage war in both philosophical and physical realms. Satan's victory will come over those who reject God in Christ in this life and die of old age, or through some evil such as 9–11, perpetrated by Satan.

Satan's promise is a gospel of self in which we simply need to tap the infinite potential that lies within and we shall be as God.

This is becoming even more obvious in this present age as we see this in much of the New Age teaching or in a religion such as the Mormon Church, which will lead many to follow the soon-appearing antichrist. Satan can transform himself as an angel of light and continues to do so to this day as Paul wrote to the Corinthian church (2 Cor. 11:3–15). This passage states not only that Eve and Satan were literal and historic persons confirming the Genesis account, but that the world would be deceived into believing that both Satan's word and man's basic righteousness is equal to God's— so who needs the Savior. Thus, we see that the stage for *the long war against God* was set from the fall of mankind (Gen. 3) to the ultimate defeat of Satan in the last days (Rev. 20).

Do we not now see why Islam would attack Israel and America? All the world recognizes the United States as a Judeo-Christian nation just as our Secretary of State Colin Powell acknowledged recently in a widely televised interview. Satan's seed in Islam is at war with the godly seed of Christ as represented by Israel and America (Rev. 12:13–17). Jesus fully understood the satanic influence behind man's actions as He acknowledged Satan's seed in the world and even called some of His fellow Jews as "of their father the devil" (Jn. 8:44). Make no doubt about it, Islam is a seed of Satan, and it is no accident that Islam is trying to paint America and Israel as satanic. We are in a holy war, whether we like it or not!

The long war against God,[7] as Dr. Henry Morris has called this struggle which was defined in the Garden of Eden, has been going on for 6000 years. Satan, the dragon of Isaiah 27:1, from the time of the warning to him in Genesis 3:15, has been on the warpath throughout history to destroy the promised *seed* of the woman, first with Abel, then the pre-flood descendants of Seth, then the seed of Abraham (Gen. 15:3–6; Gal. 3:16), the nation of Israel (this is the real root of anti-Semitism), the Son of God (the seed of the virgin and Abraham Gal. 3:16), the church of God, and eventually, all the remnant of the faithful in the great Tribulation. It would be good to take a close look at the epistle to the Galatians to see that the seed of the woman runs through Abraham to Christ. The apostle Paul writes: "Now to Abraham and his Seed were the promises made. He does not say, and to seeds, as of many, but as of one, and to your Seed, who is Christ" (Gal. 3:16). It is clear in Galatians chapter four that all those who are God's are adopted as sons (Gal. 4:5), and from the godly Abel to the last believer at the end of this age we are at war with Satan's seed. The event of 9–11 is therefore just one more battle in this satanic crusade against the people of the godly seed and their national identity that in this day resides primarily in the nations of Israel and the United States of America. Thus, the seed of Satan attacks the World Trade Center and also tries to destroy the nation of Israel.

It should be noted that the story of this pageant was given in the stars (The original twelve signs of the Mazzaroth; Gen. 1:14 and Job) to tell of the *seed* of the virgin in the constellation Virgo, and the one who would crush the head of the serpent who would bite His heel in the constellation Orion, perfectly aligning with the Genesis 3:15 text. This has been carefully spelled out in several books.[27, 28] The so-called gospel in the stars or the glory of God revealed in the heavens as Psalm 19 refers to it has been corrupted as the Scripture tells us (Rom. 1:23). But the panorama revealed to Adam and his descendants rolls on today and we are now embroiled in the last days of this long war against God! The war is in both the spiritual realm and the world (Eph. 6:11–18; 1 Tim. 1:18). The primary task for the Christian is to be prepared and to deal with the spiritual first. Ephesians 6:11–18 explains both the preparation and the battleground, which is prayer. We are called to battle, and chapter 10 will define a battle plan.

The biblically correct age of our sojourn, and the involvement of the seed of the woman and the seed of Satan in this age-long *war* that defines our history is worthy of study before we delve into the last days.

CHAPTER 5

6000-Year Time Line: As Seen by a Creation Scientist

You may indeed learn the very time when the foundation of the world was laid, if you return from the present time to former ages.
—Basil the Great, Heraemeron, A.D. 360

God is the author of time and it should not be a hard concept to comprehend that His revelation of Himself and plan for mankind includes the time schedule as well. He established time cycles (day, night, seasons, years) to facilitate His plan for His creation. Jesus even said He was the Alpha and Omega, the beginning and the end (Rev. 1:8), denoting Him as the author of time. He began with the six days of creative effort, and gave us the stars in the heavens to tell time (Gen. 1:14–18). The six-day work week, with the seventh day for rest, was for man and a sign of his creative work (Ex. 20:11). God ordained calendar feasts, and memorials (Ex. 23), the times for His program for Israel and the nations (Dan. 2:21), His Son's comings (Eph. 1:10; Heb. 1:1), the times of the Gentiles (Lk. 2:21), and the times of the end (Dan. 9–1; 1 Pet. 1:11). The last days are of particular interest in this monograph and much is clearly laid out in Scripture in both the Old and New Testaments. Jesus spoke of a period called the great Tribulation (Matt. 24:21) and Daniel and John gave the duration (Dan. 12:5–7; Rev. 11:2, 12:6, 14, 13:5). Chapter eight will spend considerable time discussing these times. With God's sovereignty over time and His revelation starting with creation and bringing us down to the end, we can agree with Basil the Great.

We who have been called creation scientists should not shy away from a reconciliation of the scientific evidence with the biblical record. Einstein, the most revered scientist of the twentieth century, understood that there was more to this world to be reconciled than just the laws of mathematics and physics. He wrote, "Everyone who is seriously interested in the pursuit of science becomes convinced that a spirit is manifest in the laws of the universe, a spirit vastly superior to man." Dr. Werner von Braun, whom I worked with in the last four years of his life, was also a Christian and a scientist who said: "One cannot be exposed to the law and order of the universe without concluding that there must be design and purpose behind it all. The better we understand the intricacies of the universe and all it harbors, the more reason we have found to marvel at the inherent design upon which it was based." Both of these men who are revered among scientists and lay people alike have been extensively quoted in the media on these topics.

One does not have to be a scientist to understand that the earth is a young planet having a cool, solid crust, a non-destructive, life-supporting atmosphere, but a molten core (Gen. 1; Ps. 33:6–10). This young earth is ideally suited for 6000 years of human habitation, but absolutely unable to exist for six billion years and be in its present state. The molten core, having no heat source, would have cooled and solidified, removing our magnetic field and its protection. The decay of our magnetic field is a well-documented fact,[8, 9] which shows both a beginning and an end time scenario which fits the biblical prophecy.

This planet is destined to be replaced or renewed in the relatively near future (Isa. 65:17; Rev. 21:1ff; 2 Cor. 4:18).

Furthermore, it will be seen that the biblical time line, the extant historical records, and the scientific evidence can be understood to agree with a period of 6000 years since God created the heavens and the earth. In short, billions of years of the earth's existence does not stand up to the biblical testimony, the secular written history, or the scientific evidence. Neither should we listen to the various positions of many Bible colleges, Christian colleges, and a vast list of churches and Christian ministries that try to allow for the position of an old earth because they can't handle science or the Scripture.

The biblical time line begins with the creation of the heavens and the earth and is easily traced from the biblical record and the secular record down to the present as we enter into the seventh millennium of our existence. Today, we have many strong arguments for accepting this time line, both from history and science. It would be good to elucidate some of these arguments for the edification of both the godly seed and the satanic seed who will read this manuscript.

Historically, the years from creation to the present may be simply added up from the data in Genesis and the rest of Scripture, and correlated with secular historical records such as the laying of the cornerstone of Solomon's temple (1 Kings 6:1) and bring the time line right up to today's calendar just as Basil and James Ussher did in their great literary works of the Fourth and Sixteenth Centuries respectively.[10] From these records we may determine: the time of creation, the Genesis flood, Babel, the days the earth was divided into the present continents, the time of Abraham, the nation of Israel, the building of Solomon's temple, the Babylonian empire, the Medo/Persian empire, the days of Alexander the Great, the Macedonian/Greek or Hellenic empire, the Roman empire, the time of Jesus the Messiah [4000 years after the Creation], and the history of our world right down to today.

The calendar that the Western world presently works with tells us we have entered into the year A.D. 2004. This calendar is based on a solar year; the A.D. stands for *Anno Domini* (year of the Lord) which is related to the birth of Christ. Dionysius Exiguus, a Sycthian monk (A.D. 525) determined that Christ was born at a date he set as A.D. 1 which was 754 years after the founding of Rome. The year and day of Christ's birth was also reported to be the twenty-fifth of Kislev (a month in the Jewish calendar which corresponds to December in the Julian and later Gregorian calendar) by Hippolytus (A.D. 165–235). Chrysostom (A.D. 345–407) wrote that December 25 was the correct date, and an early church document of A.D. 330 stated that it was thirty-three years exactly to the day from the Immaculate Conception to the crucifixion.[11] With the crucifixion coming on Passover, as all Scripture teaches, this puts the conception just nine months before December 25 and all dates begin to fit into place. More recent research into the astronomical events surrounding Christ's birth and a better understanding of Josephus' statement concerning Herod's death and the lunar eclipse before Passover have shown Christ's birth date to be 1 B.C. Ernest L. Martin, director of The Foundation for Biblical Research, Pasadena, California, published this information in an article in Christianity Today titled, *The Celestial Pagentry Dating Christ's Birth.*[12]

Dionysius was working with the Julian calendar which has since been overtaken by the Gregorian calendar. The Gregorian calendar corrected an error in the Julian calendar's length of the year, which caused an eleven-day shift when the American colonies adopted it in 1752. This calendar is the one the Western world is using today. An interesting aside here is that George Washington's birthday was listed in his mother's Bible as February 11, he being born before 1752. Afterwards George celebrated it on the twenty-second, or eleven days later.

Regarding the scientific evidence for a 6000-year biblical time line, the following are given:

The Stars, Light, and Time

Probably the most often used argument against a young earth and a biblical time line is the problem of the stars appearing to show forth their light traveling at 186,000 miles per second yielding such great distances that the time for the light to reach our observation points exceeds the 6000 time line from the creation to today as put forth in the Scripture. As noted previously in chapter two, Dr. Humphreys has tried to show compatibility with the Genesis record through gravitational time dilation (i.e. the force of gravity in large bodies of mass such as stars bend the light beam and dilate the signal, a concept that Einstein proposed in his theory of relativity). The most recent studies of the speed of light have shown that light is not bound by its formerly thought-to-be limited fixed speed of travel. These studies conducted at Princeton, NJ, where physicists sent a pulse of laser light through cesium vapor that left the chamber before it had finished entering were published in the journal *Nature*.[13] These experiments have shown that physicists have been able in laboratories to exceed the previously thought fixed speed of light by a factor of 300; other research has stopped and started light without destroying it. The biblical statement that God spread out the heavens (Job 9:8, 37:18; Ps. 104:2; Isa. 40:22, 42:5, 44:24, 51:13; Jer. 6:4, 10:12, 51:15; Zech. 12:1) precisely describes what has been demonstrated in the laboratory, i.e. that in an instant in time the light has been stretched out to the outer limits.

We have observed that the apparent relative speed of galaxies is not known by the red shift of their light spectrum as the astronomer Hubble theorized. Halton Arp, in his decades-long research on quasars, has definitely shown by the anomalies of quasars that the red shift analogy of the speed of galaxies and an expanding universe, i.e. the basis for the Big Bang theory, is a flawed theory. With several other observations denying the expanding universe theory, many have said that the Hubble law of an expanding universe is no law at all. The Big Bang theory has so many band aids on it that it can safely be said that it has been falsified. The Big Bang time scale has a serious time-light travel problem itself: there is not enough time in the hypothesis for light to travel between widely separated regions of space. There have been several attempts to cover the problem, with the most popular being the inflation hypothesis.[14] In this hypothesis, the expansion rate of the universe was vastly accelerated in an inflation phase early in the Big Bang, and the distant regions of the universe were able to come to the same temperature, as observed in the Cosmic Microwave Background radiation (CMB), before they were pushed apart at speeds faster than the speed of light. This theory, which Alan Guth of MIT devised to make the initial mass/velocity conditions of the Big Bang more plausible, is simply an attempt to save the Big Bang hypothesis, with its violation of known physical limits. In fact, it looks more like God spreading out the heavens than any naturalistic physics. The most recent attempt at resolving this enigma is a book by Joao Magueijo, a physicist at Imperial College London, titled *Faster Than the Speed of Light*.[15]

Furthermore, the amount of matter required to bring an initial explosion together by gravitational force has led Big Bang cosmologist Stephen Hawking to state that over ninety-five percent of the universe is unseen; he has concluded that it must exist as "Cold Dark Matter."[16] In other words, we can't see it or measure it, but it must exist or the known universe cannot be the product of an explosion. It takes massive amounts of matter to attract by gravitational force to bring matter together, whereas an explosion disperses matter. In addition, the position and relationship of planets in the solar system, and stars in the spinning galaxies is consistent with a young universe which has not had time to spin apart or go out of balance.

Other astronomical arguments for a younger universe than the evolutionists require, and the progressive creationists compromise the biblical record with are: 1. Missing *old* supernova remnants, and 2. Comets, which have short lives due to burn out, still existing in our solar system. These arguments are not as definitive of exactly 6000 years, but they certainly do allow for a biblical time line. Many scientific papers and books have been written in the past thirty years on these two subjects, most of which are summarized in Jonathan Sarfati's recent book *Refuting Compromise.*[63]

The Studies in Geology

The recent studies in France, Colorado State University, the Grand Canyon, Mt. St. Helens, and deep sea borings, have shown that the stratified sedimentary layers of rock were all laid down by massive water flows of varying speed and composition. These studies have shown that there is no indication of great time between the layers, and all the so-called geologic ages, as well as orogenesis (mountain building), and canyon forming, can be fit into the Genesis record of creation, catastrophism at the Flood, ice epoch, and continental division in the days of Peleg (Gen. 10:25). Some of the leaders in this research are Guy Berthault of the Geological Society in France, Steve Austin, Henry and John Morris and a host of geologists with the Creation Research Society, just to name a few leaders such as Andrew Snelling, Bernard Northrup, and Mats Molen of Sweden.[17, 18, 19]

Furthermore, the sedimentation studies of all the rivers in the world show that no river is older than 5000 years. With regard to sedimentation, the salts in the sea deny any great age for the oceans and the amounts of many of the various sediments match very closely a post-Flood time line for the current hydrological cycle. The archaeological studies of the Middle East also show a time line beginning at approximately 2400 B.C. with evidence for Noah's family, and towers (ziggurats) like the Tower of Babel with dates all less than 5000 years ago. Dr. David Livingston, founder of The Associates for Biblical Research and world renowned for his digs in Israel, has tied all of these data together into a coherent biblical time line of six thousand years.[20]

Radiometric Dating

Extensive studies are being undertaken by The Institute for Creation Research (ICR), showing that, while carbon dating of living organisms is of some accuracy back to the time of the Flood, the dating of rocks by radiometric decay is absolutely worthless. The initial radiometric condition of rocks at the time of their creation or forming from molten lava is totally unknown as to the makeup of radioactive components; rocks recently known to have been formed from volcanic activity are shown by these methods to be millions of years old. The extensive findings of these studies were presented at the Fifth International Conference on Creationism held in the Pittsburgh area in August of 2003.[19] The ICR group presented nineteen peer-reviewed papers at the conference; they were well received by the entire scientific community. One of the most significant results obtained in this research was the well-documented helium loss rate in the nuclear decay in zircons common in granitic rock. The helium loss rate is so high that almost all of it would have escaped if the uniformitarian age of the rocks of 1.5 billion years were true. But the crystals in granitic rock contain a very large amount of helium, supporting an age of only 6000 years.[21] In short, radiometric studies do not show an old earth!

Fossils

Most fossils fit nicely into a Genesis flood scenario of *rapid burial*, and long-term inundation in sedimentary rock (at least several years, but not necessarily more than a few hundred). Only this scenario is the complete solution to the great worldwide wipe out of all living creatures and their fossilization in the geologic record! Furthermore, the fossil record shows all species mature in their living form with no transitional forms, i.e. missing links, in existence as the evolutionist the late Stephen Jay Gould readily acknowledged. All life forms in the fossil record appear suddenly and fully formed at the Cambrian level of the geologic configuration.[22, 23]

DNA

DNA does not survive very long after living cells die (less than a few thousand years and sometimes less than a few hundred) yet we have found DNA in blood cells in dinosaur bones, amber nodules, and a whole host of buried, formerly living organisms that evolutionists have tried to date as millions of years old.[24] The very evolutionists who discovered these red blood cells in dinosaur bones from the Wyoming State University and Montana State University (Schweitzer and Horner) have been unable to show that these cells are not blood cells for the past six years, knowing full well the implication for an age of dinosaurs contemporary with mankind.

Population

The world population today relates to a growth from eight souls at the time of the Flood, some 4350 years ago. One of the key scientific/historical records to the veracity of Genesis is the human population of the earth, as is presented in depth in a later chapter, which agrees with the dates of the Genesis flood precisely; no million-year evolution scenario can fit these data. There are historical records of a worldwide flood in practically every ethnic group around the world.[25] There is no way to see millions of years in these data. The aforementioned later section will deal with the validity of these data.

Earth's Magnetic Field Decay

Some of the most significant of the hard scientific data for a 6000-year-old earth is the carefully measured decaying of the earth's magnetic field. The late Dr. Thomas Barnes, a professor at the University of Texas in El Paso, and author of the definitive college textbook *Foundations of Electricity and Magnetism*, showed that the measurements of the earth's magnetic field over the past 170 years show a decay rate that is totally consistent with a 6000-year-old earth. With discussions of thermodynamics, the earth's core temperatures and magnetic make up, etc. being beyond the scope of this monograph, the reader can rest assured that this earth could not have existed as a place cool enough to live on more than 10,000 years ago, and is not designed to last much longer at the rate it is decaying.

With this scientific background for holding to a biblical time line, we now shall embark on the historical record of the long war between the godly seed and the seed of Satan.

CHAPTER 6

6000 Years of Warfare

God the Creator speaking to Satan: *I will put WAR between you and the woman, between your seed and her seed . . . .*

—Gen. 3:15

God the Son speaking to His disciples: *You will hear of WARS and rumors of WARS . . . nation will rise against nation . . . .*

—Matt. 24:6–7

God in the Holy Spirit inspiring John to write: *I saw heaven opened and behold a white horse, and He who sat on him was called faithful and true, and in righteousness He judges and makes WAR.*

—Rev. 19:11

War has been ordained from the time of the fall in Genesis to the time of the end in the book of the Revelation. It could be said that *war defines our history.* The historian Tacitus wrote, "The task of history is to hold out for reprobation every evil word and deed, and to hold out for praise every great and noble word and deed." It is hoped that this chapter would so record history that it would define the difference between the good and evil and the struggle between the godly seed and the seed of

Satan that has determined the course of mankind from the days of Genesis to the present. People in the world must see war as a reality that underlies everyday life. William Bennett, author of *The Book of Virtues*, stated that this nation needs good courses in history more than it needs the preaching of values. The unity of biblical history is that man is a fallen creature whom God the creator is redeeming to create the kingdom of God. History presents us with a warfare that began in the Garden of Eden. With the curse of Genesis came the declaration of war which would dominate the panorama of history from beginning to the end of this age. Jesus said that there would be wars and rumors of wars (Matt. 24:6) throughout the period from His day until the end of the age. God prophesied war in Genesis 3, and confirmed it while He was on earth as recorded in Matthew 24. Jesus opens the seals to the final conflicts as seen by John and recorded in the Revelation chapter six. It is clear from Scripture that the godly seed is at war with the satanic seed as the apostle Paul spelled out in his letter to the Ephesians chapter 6:10–18. As pointed out in a previous chapter, Satan is going about seeking to devour the children of Adam and Eve (1 Pet. 5:8), and in the last days this infernal majesty is seen as still trying to devour the seed of the woman (Rev. 12:4). This is the biblical view of history!

Unfortunately, the Western world and primarily the dominant news people, and the secular education establishment, have destroyed much of our history and the biblical view, to the point that as a nation many don't know who we are, or where we have come from, or where we are going. I don't believe this is true of President Bush who has characterized our efforts in the Middle East as a crusade, but the public relation types stopped him from using this term. It was Henry Ford that said history is bunk; much of our modern society has adopted this philosophy. Islam, at least militant Islam, is not ignorant of their history and when they use the word *crusade* they are right back into the Seventh through the Eleventh century, still waging the war against Christendom. Islam, of course, is just one of the many faces of satanic opposition to the godly seed from the time of the fall of mankind. The satanic effort has been both on an individual level as he seeks to devour a specific person, and a corporate level such as whole nations led by whole mobs such as Hitler's mob, Stalin's mob, Mao's mob, or Saddam's mob. While it might be said that this is a narrow view of history, as everything is viewed from the perspective of Genesis 3:15, it must be stated that no view of history can ignore the impact of this true event (i.e. the fall of man and the declaration of war between the seed of the woman and the seed of Satan), and make sense of mankind's struggle and the events of 9–11. We need to see this war all the way back into history, i.e. all the way back to Genesis. With this in mind and the premise of this thesis that the 6000 years of warfare is ordained, we begin with an overview of religious history. Proceeding to an analysis of the factions and then an in-depth analysis of some of the historical record the reader can always see it as this war between the seed of the woman and the seed of Satan.

A. Overview of Biblical and Religious History

- 4000 B.C. God created the heavens and the earth in six days (Gen. 1 and 2).

- 4000 B.C. Mankind is lead into sin by Satan. All the earth is put under the curse and mankind is under a death and *war* declaration (Gen. 3:15). Abel becomes the first casualty.

- 4000 B.C.–2470 B.C. Earth reels under violence between the seed of the woman and the seed of Satan (Gen. 6).

- 2470 B.C. Noah is told of coming judgment by flood and told to build an ark (Gen. 6). The animals begin their trek across the Pangea [the entire earth a connected land mass] to Mesopotamia.

- 2350 B.C. Noah's family with the created land animals and flying creatures enter the ark and the Flood begins.

- 2351 B.C. Floodwaters recede as land is reformed by massive hydraulic forces (Gen. 8). Catastrophic filling of lakes and washouts like the Grand Canyon is characteristic of this short period of time. Runoff goes into the sea and some orogenisis occurs, but the basic Pangea remains until the days of Peleg (Gen. 10:25).

- 2281 B.C. Noah's descendants, afraid to move out over the land, are led by the rebellious Nimrod to build a tower in Babylon. God, seeing that the people have refused to obey His command to disperse and occupy the world, makes many language and ethnic changes at Babel; the nations [Gk. ethnos] are divided.

- 2217 B.C. The continents are separated in the days of Peleg after the animals have all returned to their pre-flood habitat (Gen. 10, 11) and all of the bio-geographical distribution problems regarding the Flood are answered. It should be noted that no evolutionary scenario can solve these problems.

- 2000 B.C. Noah dies and Abraham is born in Ur in Mesopotamia.

- 1950 B.C. Abraham called out of Ur to a land to be given to him by God (Gen. 12).

- 1900 B.C Abraham enters Canaan.

- 1870 B.C. Joseph, Abraham's great grandson, sold into slavery in Egypt. Israel, Joseph's father, and the rest of his family follow him into Egypt in a time of drought.

- 1500 B.C. Moses called by God.

- 1440 B.C. Israel led out of Egypt where anti-Semitism has risen in Pharaoh's heart (Ex. 1–11).

- 1400 B.C. Israel crosses the Jordan into Canaan land.

- 1000 B.C. David becomes King in Israel.

- 920 B.C. Solomon dies and the kingdom of Israel is split.

- 720 B.C. The northern kingdom is crushed and dispersed by the Assyrians from Nineveh where the heart of anti-Semitism resides in Mesopotamia to this day.

- 606 B.C. The southern kingdom is defeated by Nebuchadnezzar and Daniel is taken to Babylon.

- 586 B.C. Nebuchadnezzar returns to Jerusalem to destroy the temple.

- 539 B.C. Persia, under Cyrus, defeats Babylon and the Jews begin to return to Jerusalem just as prophesied by Isaiah 180 years before (Isa. 44:28–45:1).

- 516 B.C. Temple rebuilt and dedicated.

- 332 B.C. Alexander the Great conquers the Mediterranean and Mesopotamian world. He dies in Babylon in 321 B.C. The Greek kingdom is split between his generals just as the prophet Daniel prophesied 250 years earlier.

- 165 B.C. Jews take Jerusalem from Greeks and rededicate the temple (Hanukkah).

- 67 B.C. Rome conquers the Western world and sets up leaders in Israel.

- 1 B.C. The Son of God enters the world as the baby Jesus, the *Seed* of the woman.

- A.D. 32 The Son of God is crucified by the seeds of Satan but allowed by God to show His love for mankind and to provide a perfect way to enter into eternal life and God's kingdom (John 3:16).

- A.D. 32 The Son of God rises from the dead and ascends into heaven.

- A.D. 32 The church of Christ is born out of Judaism and begins to reach the nations of the world. A 2000-year war begins between the true church and Satan's seeds.

- A.D. 40–A.D. 70 Church moves out into all the world with many martyrs, including all the apostles, except John.

- A.D. 70 Fall of Jerusalem to Romans with the destruction of second temple. From this time to the present the true believers, the pilgrim church, becomes the focus of Satan's minions.

- What follows is a condensation of the extensive chronology of the church from A.D. 70 to A.D. 1917 as presented in the book titled *The Pilgrim Church*.[26] From A.D. 70 to A.D. 180 Ten great persecutions from Domitian to Marcus Aurelius.

- A.D. 200 Thousands of Christians martyred in Egypt.

- By A.D. 300 missionaries have gone into all the civilized world on the continents of Europe, Africa, Asia, and the Far East.

- A.D. 313 Roman Emperor Constantine gives Christianity civic recognition.

- A.D. 440–461 Papacy first formed under Leo I.

- A.D. 476 Rome falls to the Goths and Western Roman Empire comes to an end. The Western world enters the Middle Ages. The Byzantine Empire, where Constantine moved his throne in A.D. 330, lives on until A.D. 1453 when the Islamic Turks capture Constantinople.

- A.D. 622 Birth of Islam, dated from Mohammed's flight to Medina. Mohammed teaches there is no God but Allah and begins the subjection (the true meaning of Islam) of all people. In 629 Mohammed returns to Mecca with the Koran. In 637 Jerusalem falls to Caliph Omar and Caliph Abd al-Malik completes the Dome of the Rock in Jerusalem in 691. By the end of the century, Islam has swept Egypt and all of North Africa. It is prior to this that the two major factions in Islam, Shiite and Sunni, separate and cause a power struggle within Islam that exists to this day as seen in Iraq. Mohammed's grandsons, children of Fatima, Mohammed's daughter, Hassan and Hussein establish the Shiite/Fatima dynasty and although Hassan is murdered, this dynasty lives on to rule North Africa from 909 to 1171.

- A.D. 732 Battle of Tours; Charles Martel stops the advance of Islam into Europe.

- A.D. 800 Charlemagne crowned king on 25 December, and the Holy Roman Empire is now the Second Reich with the First Reich considered the Roman Empire of the time of Christ. Religious wars flare with this empire in the western world, with the seed of the woman and the seed of Satan.

- A.D. 845 Chinese Emperor Wu Tsung destroys Christian houses of worship and China embarks on centuries of isolationism.

- A.D. 1054 Catholic/Roman and Orthodox/Byzantine churches separate in what is known as the Great Schism.

- A.D. 1095 Urban II calls for a crusade to take holy sites in Palestine. This is followed by seven more crusades (until 1270).

- A.D. 1100–c. A.D. 1500 A long list of Protestant believers are martyred by the increasingly apostate Roman Catholic hierarchy. Waldensians, Huguenots, Basil, John Hus, et al., just to name a few. *Foxe's Book of Martyrs* is written in fifteenth century to show the extent of the warfare and to resist the Roman Church.

- A.D. 1199 Bosnia, which had been taken by Islam, is reached with the gospel by the Bogomils, and Christianity and Islam are recorded over and over through the centuries at war in these areas. It was really a reversal of roles when NATO, with the backing of the Clinton administration, attacked the Christian Serbs, and protected the Islamic (so-called *ethnic* by the liberal press) Bosnian/Albanians.

- A.D. 1258 Baghdad is captured by the Mongols under Genghis Kahn; tolerant of Christians, he is intent on the destruction of Islam.

- A.D. 1368 Fall of the Mongol Empire; rise of the Ming Dynasty in China.

- A.D. 1389 Battle of Kosovo extends Turkish rule over Serbia. Severe persecution in Bosnia forces 40,000 Bogomils to flee.

- A.D. 1453 Constantinople and Eastern Roman Empire captured by Muslim Turks. City renamed Istanbul.

- A.D. 1400–1600 Tares, i.e. bad seeds, in Christianity in the Roman Church and other apostates are at war with the true seed in the pilgrim church throughout Western civilization.

- A.D. 1492 Christopher Columbus reaches the New World; Spanish Inquisition removes all Muslims and Jews from Spain.

- A.D. 1517 Martin Luther discovers salvation by grace through faith and the Reformation breaks forth under Luther, Calvin, Swingli, Knox et al. which changes the face of Christianity.

- A.D. 1620 Mayflower carrying 102 Pilgrims (Puritan separatists) sail from Plymouth England to America.

- A.D. 1642 Civil war in England. Cromwell, Puritan MP, defeats the monarchy and becomes Lord Protector.

- A.D. 1618–1648 Thirty Years War in Europe.

- A.D. 1653 Protestants in England given religious liberty.

- A.D. 1500–1700 Catholics and Protestants of several stripes continue to war against each other in places as diverse as Europe, England, and as far away as China.

- A.D. 1776 American colonies declare independence from England and establish a Judeo-Christian republic unique in all the world.

- A.D. 1800s Satan has an outpouring of activity with the establishment of cults in America (Mormon 1830; Spiritualism 1848; Jehovah's Witnesses 1872; Christian Science 1876).

- A.D. 1895 Turks massacre 300,000 Christian Armenians.

- A.D. 1901 Boxer Rebellion in China feeds anti-West sentiments; thousands of Christians, both missionaries and nationals, are killed.

- A.D. 1914–1918 WW I, 1939–1945 WW II, sets the scene for the present world situation and the final assault of the satanic world powers on the bastions of Judeo-Christianity.

- A.D. 1948 The nation of Israel is created in the biblical homeland of the Jews.

- A.D. 1948 Rise of Islamic opposition to Israel and the beginning of militant terrorism against Jews and Christians that is demonstrated in 9–11.

- Today, the present worldwide Jihad is ever growing in the clash of civilizations which characterize the last days of this age as the Bible has prophesied.

With this abbreviated overview the following sections will attempt to see behind the scenes so that we might better understand the world at war today. The present conflict is really just the last days in a six-millennium battle which has its roots in the scene from the third chapter of Genesis.

B. Factions in this Long War

In the annals of mankind the seed of Satan has been manifested in a variety of individuals and a variety of socio-religious movements, all of which show enmity towards the godly seed of the woman. The warring factions break very simply into two camps or two spiritual races defined from Genesis 3:15, both descended from Adam and Eve. The seed of the woman as seen in Abel, and the seed of the serpent as seen in Cain, can be traced down through history as *the long war against God* is carried on to this day with the events of 9–11.

1. The godly *seed* is made up of all of the redeemed who have been saved by the atoning sacrifice of the seed of the woman who is Jesus God's Son. This preeminent *Seed* of the woman, looked forward to in the Genesis passage, is the man/God Jesus the Christ just as the Scripture tells us (Gal. 3:16–19). All of the rest of the godly seed are Eve's descendants who have believed God and thus are saved by faith (Heb. 11). This godly seed, who were all dead in Adam (Rom. 5:12), are now alive by Christ (Rom. 5:14–21; 1 Cor. 15:45). All are sinners both by nature and act, such as Abel, Noah, Abraham, Jacob, King David, Saul the chief of sinners who became Paul, John Newton (the author of the hymn *Amazing Grace*), and myself. This group is not organizationally identified, as in any organization there are true believers and false professors as indicated by the parable of the wheat and the tares (Matt. 13:24). God did not create a man-ruled organization that we are to join to be related to Him. It is directly by faith that we come into an eternal relation to God and become joint heirs with Christ (Rom. 8:14–17; Eph. 2:8–10, and many other passages). The tares are all the unsaved, including those who are generally considered as apostates, heretics, cults, etc. who claim to be Christian, but in many cases are the satanic seeds masquerading in the hierarchy of the church as could be seen from the historical record of *The Pilgrim Church*. Paul warned Timothy about these, and Jude spoke of them. If one wants to try to identify the wheat, the book of 1 John is a good guide.

2. The *seed* of Satan is made up of those who reject the Creator and His Son. This involves a long list of variants as

we shall see in the time line. Jesus acknowledged their existence as well as their heritage as recorded in John 8:44, where He identifies those of His Jewish kin who wanted to kill Him as being "of their father the devil." Many of these are readily identified such as idol worshippers, animists, Buddhists, Confucianists, Taoists, Hindus, Muslims of all variations, godless atheists, Communists, Fascists, evolutionists, secular humanists, many in the name of religion, even pseudo or cultic Christianity, or just evil individuals in all societies as attested to by the evening news most every day. Every generation is confronted with satanic movements that seek to destroy life, freedom, and the godly seed.

The particular efforts of Satan have always been to destroy the path of God's creation to His kingdom. So Abel is slain, and only a remnant of Abraham's seed made it through to the birth of Jesus the Messiah. The Scripture tells us that Jesus was tempted in this life to accept the satanic realm of this present world (Matt. 4) and thus Satan had hoped to destroy the seed of the woman in Christ. The Scripture tells us just how perverse people are entered into by Satan and they become the *seed of Satan* as is related in the tale of *Judas Iscariot* in John chapter thirteen. It was said of Judas by Christ that Judas's heel would be against Christ that the "Scripture might be fulfilled" (Jn. 13:18). Just what Scripture was fulfilled was of course Genesis 3:15 where the seed of Satan was said to bruise "the heel" of the seed of the woman. John tells us that Satan entered in to Judas and Judas immediately went out into the night to betray Jesus (Jn. 13:27–30). Thus Judas is seen as the archetypical seed of Satan. But Jesus prevailed against the evil one in this life only to be nailed to a cross and slain by the evil one's people. But God raised His Son from death, and now the believers in Christ's life, death, and resurrection, having put our trust in His completed atonement for our relationship to God and eternal life, have become the seeds of God, i.e. the woman. Thus, it is seen that it is the evil one's plan that Christians are slain, and modern Israel is to be eradicated. In all of these efforts Satan is ultimately defeated by God's chosen seed, the seed of the woman, His Son (Gal. 3:16) who was raised from death into eternal life (1 Cor. 15). It could be said that when Satan slays his own, such as the great wars of history or a Palestinian suicide bomber, then Satan is victorious as he has claimed some permanently for his infernal kingdom.

With regard to evaluating who or what constitutes the *seed* of Satan, it should be said that any religion or cult that does not provide an all-sufficient savior and salvation from the curse of Genesis 3:15, including the removal of the guilt and power of sin, and able to deliver one to an eternal position with the Creator *is* Satanic. *The seed of the woman, Jesus, God's only begotten Son*, alone provides this deliverance. Scripture states that, "There is no other name under heaven given among men whereby we must be saved" (Acts 4:12; Isa. 43:11).

The Scripture is clear on who is energizing the people involved in the wars of history, and who will be involved in energizing the participants in the last days. Paul writes in 2 Thessalonians 2:9–12 that Satan is working (Gk. *evergeiav*, i.e. *energizing*) in the antichrist who is coming and in all who have not believed the truth of the gospel. This is opposed to God who is energizing all who believe in Him and the Lord Jesus the Christ, God's Son (Phil. 2:13). Thus, we see the powers behind this long war just as Genesis 3:15 stated, that define world history. It has been said that life takes its own turns, makes its own demands, writes its own story, and along the way we realize that we are not the author; truly we are being energized by powers outside our realm. Can there be any greater revelation to see the need for prayer? All this will remain the case, given the fallen nature of man and the limited dominion of Satan in this age, until the advent of the messianic age, which will bind Satan and the kingdom of God will reign in peace on Earth (Rev. 20).

C. Chronological History of the War in Depth

We have shown, both scientifically and historically, that it is rational to believe in a literal and historical Genesis account. Not only is it rational to believe in a six-day creation, but we have also shown that it is rational to believe in a six-thousand-year time line since God created Adam and Eve (4000 B.C.). That this pair were deceived by Satan has been clearly explained in the previous chapter; this world has been in a kingdom creating and war-like mode ever since. The kingdoms are the kingdom of God, which will be manifested in the coming age, and the kingdom of Satan, which will be bound in the millennial age and sentenced to its final abode in the eternal state. The six millennia of world history which have preceded this day have been characterized by this *long war against God* of which 9–11 is a defining event in these last days of this longest war.

Abel, the first casualty of the war, called one of a cloud of martyrs in Hebrews 12:1, was slain by his brother Cain as the scriptural record tells us, a record probably written by Adam (Gen. 5:1), and later written by Moses. Abel obviously knew the gospel of the blood atonement, having offered a lamb, but Cain had taken the position of Satan that his works would be accepted by God. When God told him that this was not acceptable (Gen. 4:7), it is obvious God had taught the children of Adam that only a blood sacrifice, as Abel offered, was acceptable for man's fallen condition, Cain rose up in anger and slew God's accepted child, his brother Abel (Gen. 4:3–7) and the war began.

It should be clearly understood that God had told Adam and Eve and their children of His great plan of redemption. This plan was apparently signed in the stars as Genesis 1:14 declares. This plan, which focuses on the virgin-born *seed* seen in the constellation *Virgo*, progresses throughout the history of the *long war* as the serpent attacks the heel of Orion and Orion slays the head of the dragon just as Genesis 3:15 predicted, and culminates in the triumph of *Leo, the lion of the tribe of Judah*. This entire story was laid out in the zodiac, which was told to every man from Adam to Moses until the story is corrupted by the ancient philosophers after the Flood. This is all spelled out in my book titled *Specific Revelation: The Gospel prior to Moses* (27, 28).

Eve's third child Seth was born, and it was through him that the world began to call upon *Yahweh* as the Creator (Gen. 4:26). But things were not peaceful on planet Earth as the war between Satan's seed and the godly seed waged on. Satan had led a third of the host of heaven in his rebellion; some of these *nephilim* (Gen. 6:2) even invaded earth and took many women for themselves. The pre-flood world was characterized by *warfare* and violence (Gen. 6:13); it was at this point that God set the date of the Genesis flood (Gen. 6:3). The Genesis flood is well documented in both the secular, geologic, and biblical record. It should be noted that Jesus, Peter, and Paul all referred to these events and people (Matt. 19; 24, 2 Pet. 3, Rom. 5). From Abel to Noah, the wars on earth, with violence becoming the dominating scenario, caused God to judge the world with a worldwide flood (Gen. 6–9) which was to stand as a testimony that God will bring the final judgment to complete this dispensation (2 Pet. 3).

With the post-flood era, which should be dated from 2350 B.C., the family of Noah began to populate the world and bring God's plan to fruition. As Noah's family moved onto the plain between the two rivers (Mesopotamia) a very different spirit rose up in

Nimrod. He convinced the people to build a tower and stick together under his domain in a city that would be named Babel. There is much speculation as to what inspired the building of the tower, the remains of which exist to this day. Some have said it was to worship the stars from a lofty position up in their domain, and others have said it was to provide a center focus for Nimrod's leadership of Noah's descendants, but it may be that this was a vision given by Satan to Nimrod regarding the configuration of the eternal city whose builder and maker is God (Heb. 11:10; Rev. 21–22), and thereby Nimrod could take on a name for himself equal to God. This is the judgment of God when it happened, so He confused their language and thereby caused the immediate scattering of the nations into all the world (Gen. 11). It was this event that fundamentally gave us the ethnic groups we see throughout the world today.

Nimrod-bar-Cush was the apostate leader of his generation, the seed of Satan who spawned religious wars from his day to our present day. J. Dwight Pentecost, in his book *Things to Come*, records that ancient lore tells us that Semiramis, the wife of Nimrod, was the founder of Babylonian mystery religion and the fountainhead of idolatry, the mother of every heathen and pagan system in the world.[29] Building on the primeval promise of the woman's Seed who was to come, Semiramus bore a son whom she declared was miraculously conceived! This son, Tammuz, was presented to the people as the promised deliverer. Thus was introduced the mystery religion of the mother and child which is seen in Astoreth and Tammuz in Phoenicia, Isis and Horus in Egypt, Aphrodite and Eros in Greece, Venus and Cupid in Italy and bore many other names throughout the world.

Two generations later, in the days of Peleg, God divided the earth into the present continents (Gen. 10:25), creating the biogeographical distribution that we see today. Peleg, who was born two generations after Babel and Nimrod, is named for a word which means *divided by water*.[30] This was some 103 years after the Flood. Thus, it gave the animals time to return to their pre-flood locations before the breakup of the continents, which was just the same amount of time they had to come to the ark, when Noah was told to start construction. This moderately cataclysmic event of the continents moving was not only noted in Scripture (Gen. 10:25; 1 Chron. 1:19), but apparently Plato was referring to it as he described the continent of Atlantis moving away from Africa and Europe in this time.[31] This solves many bio-geographical problems regarding: the continent of Australia, the three-toed sloth in South America, and the DNA of some American natives matching Africa and Europe, and some Native American's DNA matching Asians. It also tells us that not all of the continent shaping and orogenesis occurred in the Flood or in the year or so immediately following the Flood. Thus, we can see the ark resting on a markedly more gentle mountain than that of the present condition of Ararat.[32]

With the division of continents, and the ethnic/language division, the present world was set up by God for the years of conflict between the evil seeds of Satan and the godly seeds manifested in His chosen people. The chosen people are all those who understand God's redemption through the atonement of His Son and who chose to believe it as God's provision for the problem that began in Genesis 3. Since this revelation was initially spelled out in the stars it is not surprising that Satan's first attack in this era is the corruption of the zodiac. Prior to the calling of Abraham we see the rise of Babylon, Assyria, and Egypt in the Middle East. These nations are forever to be the ones who lead the anti-Semitic efforts to destroy the chosen seed and corrupt the zodiac in their astrology.

It is interesting to see what happened in the Far East as a vacuum in godly revelation lead to some of the most bizarre creations of the satanically deceived human mind—Hinduism, Confucius, Buddha, and other animistic, and philosophical bents such as Taoism, Shintoism etc. The oldest of these is Hinduism, which arose in the Indus valley civilization shortly after the Tower of Babel dispersion of 2300 B.C.

Hinduism is so unlike any other religion that it is difficult to define theologically with any precision. It has no founder. Its precise origins have eluded scholars and other investigators. What is known for certain is that there was a highly developed civilization in the Indus valley from about 2200 B.C. (just after the time of Babel). The term *Hindu* derives from an ancient Sanskrit term meaning *dwellers by the Indus River*. The doctrines of the religion are derived from several writings such as the Rig Veda, and other Vedas circa 1300 B.C. which are supplemented by the writings called the Brahmans added to the Vedas circa 700 B.C. with the Aranyakas and the Upanishads between 600 and 300 B.C.

With this diverse set of teachings, it is not practical to define a systematic theology for Hinduism. However, there are several features of Hinduism which are more or less universal, and bring it into direct conflict i.e. *war*, with Christianity. These teachings are reincarnation, the caste system, the sanctity of the Ganges River, a multiplicity of gods such as Vishnu, Shiva, Brahma, Krishna, and the mother goddess Shakti, and the Aryan beliefs which Adolph Hitler was so enamored with. It is also noted that Margaret Sanger, the founder of Planned Parenthood, held and advocated these same Aryan views, advocating the extinction of the mentally deficient just as Hitler consigned these same people to extinction. Hitler's involvement with the occult extended to the deities as seen in the Roman Pantheon, a 2000-year-old building in Rome, which has the exact symbols laid out on one wall with the eagle and the swastika as Nazi Germany had on its banners. It is easy to see the satanic seed in these systems and the wars that have come from these people over the years. Recent conversion to Christianity by many of the untouchables in India in 2003 has led to their death at the hands of Hindu fanatics. We could also cite the murder of many Christian missionaries over the years by Hindu mobs, the most recent occurring in 2004.

The book of Job gives much insight to the role of Satan in this world and his destructive power over the godly seed. It also gives some great insights into the creation as well as defining some creatures which were probably dinosaurs (Job 40). The book of Job dates from around 2000 B.C. which places Job as a contemporary of Abraham, the progenitor of the nation of Israel.

From the Babylonian mystery religion in Mesopotamia, the patriarch Abraham was separated by divine call. The nation that sprang from him in Isaac and Jacob has been in conflict with this evil seed ever since. The ages of anti-Semitism, as documented in Richard Gade's book *A Historical Survey of Anti-Semitism*,[60] is nothing more than the long history of the war between the seeds of Satan and the seeds of the woman. That the progenitor of the Arabs, Ishmael, was an illegitimate seed of Abraham is seen as a time bomb waiting to explode, and must be seen as Satan appealing to man's sin-cursed nature to achieve his ends. Satan, ever the deceiver, even polluted the northern kingdom of Israel with Baal worship in the days of Ahab and spread this idolatry to Judah until the Babylonian captivity. When the city of Babylon was destroyed by the Medes and the Persians, and the Jews returned to Jerusalem, it is said that the high priests of Babylon's mystery religion fled to Pergamos where the symbol of the *serpent* was set up as the emblem of hidden wisdom. The ancient cult was propagated under the name of Etruscan Mysteries and eventually the Roman Empire became the headquarters of Babylonianism. Long before Christ and the days of the church at Rome, Italy became tainted by this religion. The chief priest of this mystery religion when established at Rome took the title Pontifex Maximus. When Julius Caesar was elected head of state in 167 B.C. he took this title; it was held by all Roman emperors down to Constantine who was the first Christian to rule Rome. How this relates to the present Roman Catholic Church is not up for examination in this work, but the many wars in the Western world between this Roman system and the *Pilgrim Church* manifested in the true believers wrought terror and dark ages until the great reformation of the sixteenth century brought in a measure of deliverance to the Western world.

Returning to the spiritual vacuum that was India and China, i.e. the Far East, it is interesting to note that there were several efforts to create peace by man's teaching which is always a delusion for fallen man, considering the mandate for Satan in Genesis 3:15. We would certain classify Buddhism and Zoroastrianism in the fifth and sixth century B.C. as these kind of efforts, as well as Confucianism, Taoism, and Shintoism. A brief study of the life of the Buddha is sufficient to explain this delusion. In 563 B.C. a Hindu prince was born named Siddhartha Guatama. He was to be called the Buddha meaning *the enlightened one*. The Buddha was born to a noble family in Lumbini in what is now southwestern Nepal. This young prince was raised in luxury by an adoring father who sought to protect him from the knowledge and sight of evil. The tradition goes that one day as a young man he rode forth from the palace in his chariot. By the roadside he saw an old man, a sick man, and a corpse on a litter. Shocked by this confrontation with death, sickness, etc. the prince lost all joy in living. Renouncing the ways of the world, he sought to gain insight into life's meaning through penance, fasting, and meditation as he sat under the Bo tree. After an extended time with this regimen, he said he had a spiritual awakening, and began to teach that there is a middle way to life's extremes of indulgence and mortification. This middle way involved Four Noble Truths, which are mediated by following the

Noble Eightfold Path of right views, right aspirations, right speech, right behavior, right mode of livelihood, right efforts, right thoughts, and right contemplation. Man was to do no harm to any creature. Expressly forbidden were theft, lying, unchastity, strong drink, and taking of life. Thus, man can save himself from this world's evils. Buddhism has no creation, no beginning, no end, no heaven, and no revelation from God in its teaching. Buddha became famous and was followed for his teaching and holiness. He died around 483 B.C. at the age of eighty; his followers number in the millions today. All of these Far Eastern movements, while advocating peace, are really at war with God the Creator and Redeemer of mankind. It is sufficient to note regarding Buddhism, and their false portrayal in today's press as a peaceful movement, that in A.D. 1637 it was the Buddhists in Japan that instigated some 100,000 soldiers to wipe out the remnant of Christianity in Japan.[33] Furthermore, just to see that this war is always Satan's war against the seed (Gen. 3:15; Gal. 3:16), the Zen Buddhist priests during World War II were not only guaranteeing passage to paradise to kamikaze pilots in Japan, but in 1943, Hakuun Yasutani, a major proponent of Zen Buddhism, wrote a book expressing hatred for "the scheming Jews."[34]

With the rise of the Medo-Persian Empire in 539 B.C. God began to work with His prophets to set the stage for the fullness of time to bring His Son into the world, the *Seed* of the woman, and the Lion of the tribe of Judah. Daniel the prophet, in captivity in Babylon, foretold of the fall of Babylon and the coming kingdoms of Persia, Greece, and Rome. Alexander the Greek, having conquered Persia, tried to conquer India but was decimated by the vastness of the country. Upon the death of Alexander in Babylon at the age of thirty-three in 321 B.C., his empire was divided amongst his generals into four kingdoms as accurately predicted by Daniel over two centuries earlier.

Antiochus Epiphanies, the grandson of one of Alexander's generals, in 168 B.C., became the fulfillment of the prophecy of Daniel (Dan. 9:24–27) which was given in Babylon circa 580 B.C. Antiochus' desecration of the temple instigated the revolt that brought Judaism back into control of Jerusalem in preparation for the advent of God's Son, Jesus the Messiah (Hebrew: *Yeshua Ha Maschiach*). Thus, Antiochus was the precursor of the final antichrist who again would be an abomination in Jerusalem prior to the second coming of Jesus (Matt. 24:15).

After the Jews regained Jerusalem from the Greeks, the Roman Empire rose to power over the Western world and soon brought much of Europe, Africa, Asia, and the Middle East including Judea into what was called *Pax Romana*. We have already reviewed the religious background of the Roman Empire, and it was into this scenario that Jesus the Son of God was born in Bethlehem. His life, death, and resurrection are well documented in the Bible, both prophetically and historically. When Jesus ascended into heaven with the promise to send power to His disciples (Matt. 28:18–20; Jn. 14:25–29; Acts 1:8) the gospel of Christ quickly spread throughout the world. A very interesting observation should be made with regard to God dealing with the spread of the gospel into the Western world, which sets up the present conflict. In the apostle Paul's call to reach the Gentiles (Acts 13:47) we see God, through the Holy Spirit, turning Paul to the West (Acts 16:6) and forbidding him to preach the word in Asia. This, as previously mentioned, has left the Far East for the most part in the darkness of Hinduism, Buddhism, and an easy conquest for Islam. By contrast, the Western World has become a haven for Christianity. Europe, and particularly France, has been a battleground between true believers, and the forces of evil in its many aspects over the centuries. It is not therefore surprising that in these last days France is without a heart for facing down the root of evil. From the days of the Huguenots, through the Reformation when Calvin left Paris for Geneva, the American Revolution, the Nazi/Vichy government, to the present crisis in IRAQ, France has shown itself to be a nation without direction. John Adams correctly characterized France in 1781 as a world absorbed in its own selfish lust.[35] Adams, as ambassador to France in the days leading up to the French Revolution, could not accept the idea of reason being enshrined as a religion and said, "I know not what to make of a republic of thirty million atheists."[36]

Going back to the early church, the spirit of the evil one has created many tares in the church such as the Gnostics that Paul dealt with. As the centuries went by there were Manichaeism, Arianism, Pelagianism, and Sacerdotalism just to name a few. On the other hand, Athanasius and Augustine stand out as pillars in the *Pilgrim Church* with a specific call for the needs of the time. This is not to say that everything they wrote or said would be considered perfectly biblical by this or any theologian, but God had His purposes in these men which drove the church and even Columbus to the new world. It was this new world with its Puritans, Pilgrims, and many other Christian faces which eventually brought us to today as being the defining national face of the seed of the woman. This means that the USA is now the focus of the evil one for attack. Whether it be in our national mores, as exemplified by the Clintons or the entertainment world, or as a nation opposed to Islamic fundamentalism, we are in a *War*.

At this point it would do well to take a more in-depth look at Islam. Islam was founded by the prophet Mohammed. In A.D. 610 he spent six months in a cave, and came out telling all who would listen that he had received a message from God, whom he called Allah. Mohammed then proceeded to reveal one revelation after another over the next twenty-odd years, which were written down by various scribes, since Mohammed was illiterate. Robert Morey in his book *The Islamic Invasion*[37] explains that Mohammed's revelations were a mixture of persuasion, irrational ramblings, mighty claims, contradictions of the biblical record, and in the final analysis, a declaration of war on all who did not submit to the socioreligious rule of Islam. These so-called revelations were written by Mohammed's followers in a book called the Quran (Koran) which was said to be inscribed on tablets in heaven from the beginning of time. To say that Islam is a religion of peace is nonsense. The word *Islam* means *submission*.

Just a few samples of some of the submission/war commands from the Koran are:

Sura (chapter) 2.189 and Sura 8.40 both state: Fight against the idolaters until idolatry is no more and Allah's religion reigns supreme.

Sura 9.41: Whether unarmed or well equipped, march on and fight for the cause of Allah . . .

Sura 9.73: O Prophet, make war on the unbelievers and hypocrites and deal rigorously with them; their home shall be Hell . . .

Sura 25.54: Do not yield to unbelievers, but strive against them in a strenuous Jihad.

Several other *war* verses could be cited, but we can see that Muslims who make up one fifth of the world's population are bent on subjecting their rule over all of mankind. They have been involved in three-quarters of the inter-civilizational wars in the past decade. Although much of the satanic seed abides in many cultures, it is seen that the Muslim religion is by far the most violent, and we should not be surprised that 9–11 came to America through Islam in these last days.

Islam from A.D. 632 to present represents almost 1500 years of imperialistic, colonialist, bloody conquest which has revived in the last days to give us 9–11 and the terrorists within Israel and around the world. The worldwide conquest started by Mohammed was successful in the Middle East, Africa, and into the fringes of the Western world. The Christian West first defeated Islam in Europe through Charles Martel in the battle of Tours in A.D. 732. El Cid in Spain gave the Spanish Catholics the power to evict the Moors forever, and the last Muslim ruler of Granada, Boabdil, handed over the keys to the city in 1492 to Ferdinand and Isabella. Vienna, besieged for the first time in 1529 by an immense Turkish/Muslim army, was saved when all Christian Europe, including the Spaniards, rallied to Charles V's appeal for help. The Turks withdrew from Central Europe and became an off-again on-again problem to the west and Christianity to this day. When the Hungarians, Russians, and other Christian forces defeated Islamic forces, mostly constituted in the Turkish invaders, Islam slowed down its worldwide ambitions and tried to paint itself as benign members of a secular world. But the *evil one* is not asleep and the current revival of world conquest can be traced to the rise of Wahhabism.

Mohammed Ibn Abd-al-Wahhab (d. 1792) advocated that the true Islamic faith was one committed to his teaching and a return to global purity and domination by Islam. Dore Gold in his book *Hatred's Kingdom*[38] documents the teaching and rise of Wahhabism in the Arab nations. The most significant adoption of Wahhabism has occurred in the Al Said family that currently rules Saudi Arabia. This family swore allegiance to Wahhabism over a century before their current kingdom in Saudi Arabia was realized. It was the leadership of this family that overthrew the Turks in World War I, that backed and banked the Islamic takeovers in Afghanistan and Chechnya, and is primarily responsible for the trouble in the Balkans and Lebanon and last of all the treachery of 9–11. Osama bin Laden is Wahhabi and part of the Saudi family. Saddam Hussein is Wahhabi. The terrorist group called Hammas is Wahhabi, but the most frightening revelation is that most all of the mosques in the United States (now almost 2000) are funded by Arab oil from Saudi Arabia with Wahhabi Imams in control of the teaching.

Finally, in dealing with these troubled times, which I believe to be the final days in the clash of civilizations and the remaking of world order, we certainly need to understand Islam. The world-renowned historian S. P. Huntington of Harvard has cataloged the 1990s as a period of intense antagonisms and violent conflicts between Muslims civilizations and non-Muslims and defined a future scenario where civilizations are replacing nations.[39] Just to list some of the violent conflict areas: Bosnian Muslims versus orthodox Serbs; Kosovar Albanian Muslims versus Serbs and the Macedonian Greeks; Turks versus Greeks in Cyprus; Turks versus Armenia; Muslims against China; Pakistan Muslims versus Hindu India; Muslims against Buddhists in Bangladesh; Muslims against Christians in Sudan, Indonesia, Philippines, Lebanon, Ethiopia, Nigeria and just about anywhere you can find them. Muslims against Russia in Chechnya and Afghanistan; and last, but not least, Muslims against the nation of Israel. So again we see Islam as the leading force as the *seed* of Satan against the *seed* of the woman in Christian believers, Jews where ever they are, as well as any people not in submission to Islamic rule.

Of course, it is not just Islam in the *War* against God's people. As the twentieth century, ushered in with the attempt to exterminate the Christian religion in China by the Empress Tzu Hsi, we have seen a century of martyrdom unprecedented in all of history by the sheer numbers of those slain by the seeds of Satan. China under communism should have a special mention here. Since Mao took over China after World War II, there has been a concerted effort to wipe out Christianity in the land. With thousands murdered, and hundreds of thousands in over 1100 slave labor camps, producing goods to sell to the Western world, communist China, right up to this very day is one of the greatest satanic seeds.[40] The *Long War against God* has thus expanded in the twentieth century through many seeds of Satan in the natives of Africa, and New Guinea, in the Japanese in Manchuria and Korea, the Turks in Armenia, the communists in Russia, Eastern Europe, south-east Asia as well as China, and the Germans in World Wars I and II in Europe, just to name a few.

R. J. Rummel, a University of Hawaii political science professor, in his book *Death by Government*, has documented the fact that during the twentieth century, 203 million people were killed by their own governments through war and mass killings. Citing Russia, Communist China, Nazi Germany, Cambodia, Vietnam, North Korea, and others, Professor Rummel zeros in on Islamic Turkey which massacred an estimated 1.5 million Armenian Christians between 1915 and 1923, a story which is currently being made into a movie. Fighting Satan in the twentieth century has involved a long list in a rogues' gallery that includes satanic leaders and philosophical change agents who are responsible for the greatest century of death and destruction ever foisted on mankind. Just to name a few of the leaders of this twentieth century holocaust the following are cited: Adolph Hitler, Mussolini, J.V. Stalin, Mao Tse Dung, V.I. Lenin, Pol Pot, Khrushchev, Fidel Castro, Kim il Sung, Ho Chi Minh, Kwame Nkrumah, Patrice Lumbumba, Idi Amin, and Yomo Kenyatta. Moving on to Islam, listing: Khomeini of Iran, Muammar el-Qaddafi of Libya, Hafez el-Assad of Syria, and finally the most violent Islamic devils are Yasser Arafat, Saddam Hussein, and Osama bin Laden who brought us 9–11. Nor should we overlook the philosophical agents who have backed and inspired these leaders: Joseph Goebbels, Karl Marx, Fredrich Engels, Nietzsche, Margaret Sanger, John Dewey, Jean Paul Sarte, Alfred Kinsey, Charles Darwin, and the list goes on. All of these seeds of Satan have brought upon the world untold death, misery, and bloodshed. The *International Religious Freedom Report* published by the U.S. State Department documents this warfare primarily in terms of how the world treats Christianity. The 2003 report gave an increasing list of violations in the countries of Burma, Belarus, Brunei, China, Cuba, Egypt, Eritrea, Georgia, Indonesia, Iran, North Korea, Pakistan, Saudi Arabia, Sudan, and Vietnam. North Korea was especially pointed out as executing and torturing Christians. There is ample evidence for the world and our liberal media to say that there is a *war* being waged against Judeo-Christianity on a global scale. Furthermore, it is time for our national leaders, both church and political, to tell our world just what is really behind this *war*. It is obvious to all who wish to see the difference between Christianity, which has brought peace and freedom to civilization, and the seeds of Satan which have brought six millennia of war to mankind.

Now, in the last days of this dispensation, something has happened that should tell us that the times of the Gentiles is about over (Lk. 21:24). In 1948 the nation of Israel was reborn after a 2000-year hiatus from the land. If Satan was ever more active than now to foster anti-Semitism, it certainly could be said that the twentieth century, with the Holocaust of the Second World War and the Arab world trying to destroy Israel and the United States, has shown the Bible believing world that we are in *the last days of the longest war.*

In the last half of the twentieth century, Islam has revived to declare Jihad (holy war) and eliminate Israel and their Christian allies. Satan is trying to prevent the fulfilling of the prophecy in Zechariah 12:10, where Israel will look upon Christ whom they pierced and repent. This will take place at the return of the crucified one. Modern-day Islam is not only Satan's tool to destroy modern day Israel but to this day the slaughter of Christians goes on around the world. Paul Marshall in his book *Their Blood Cries Out,*[61] spells out a long litany Satan's seeds slaughtering Christians around the world in the following areas: *Jihad* in Sudan, Iran, Saudi Arabia, Pakistan, Egypt, Algeria, Morocco, Turkey, Kuwait, Brunei, Bangladesh, Malaysia, Indonesia, Philippines, East Timor, West Africa including Nigeria, East Africa, and Central Asia; *Communism* in China, North Korea, Cuba, and Vietnam; *Hinduism and Buddhist groups* in India, Sri Lanka, Nepal, Bhutan, Burma, and Cambodia, just to name the most significant. Just to highlight the true nature of this war against Christianity, we can look at Indonesia. Indonesia is the world's fourth largest nation and the world's largest Muslim nation. The International Christian Concern foundation of Washington D.C. has documented that in the last seven years in Indonesia 80,000 Christian homes have been burned down, 1000 churches destroyed and approximately 10,000 Christians murdered and tens of thousands wounded. Dr. Marshall blames the Western media, academia, secular evolutionists, and the World Council of Churches for their apathy in not dealing with the problem. It also appears that the CIA might have seen 9–11 coming if they had read Marshall's book, or understood what Samuel Huntington was postulating in his book *The Class of Civilizations*.

Not to be overlooked is the spiritual decline in the Western world, which is seen in the immorality in the entertainment media, on the internet, the daily crime reports, etc. Today, in the Western world, there is a plethora of false religious systems which are briefly noted as: ET/SETI/UFOs, Wicca, Possibility Thinking and a whole host of ancillary groups, not the least of which is the dominant philosophy of naturalism, taught by the high priests of science, which is a religion in and of itself as documented by many credible studies by men such as Dr. Henry Morris, Dr. John MacArthur, and testified to in the recent Arkansas creationism trial. Neither should we overlook the Masonic orders in the free world which the author Stanley Monteith has characterized in his book titled the *Brotherhood of Darkness* as the moving force behind globalization and the new world order.[41]

Before we go into the eschatology of the last days of this cosmic battle, as will be covered in chapter 8, it would be profitable to take a studied and scientific look at the present and coming days to see just what a secular approach is worth regarding our efforts. In short, can mankind with his scientific and humanitarian efforts, bring peace to this world?

CHAPTER 7

A Scientific Look at the Uncertain Future

The Great World Disorder (Le Grande Disordre Mondial), Paris, 2002). Title of a book by Sergio Romano, former Italian ambassador in Moscow.

A realist from the secular world, Sergio Romano, has painted what has been called the bleakest picture of the future as we experience the last days of what Professor Samuel Huntington has called *The Clash of Civilizations*. Can we overcome the war scenario that has been our lot since the evil one declared war on the seed of the woman? Well, if you listen to some of the globalists among us you might say so. So let's examine their evidence.

It has been said by former vice president Al Gore that, "We can solve tomorrow's problems with tomorrow's technology." In his politically correct environmentalist book *Earth in the Balance*[42] Gore enters into a biased pseudoscientific world of *globalist* government that is purported to solve the needs of this planet for peace and prosperity for the next millennium. These globalist environmentalists are totally ignorant of the planet's real problem, i.e. that we all lie in Adam and are under the influence of the evil one (Satan).

The globalists in the Western world, while often suppressing unfavorable scientific data, emphatically cite a whole list of issues such as famine, wars, drugs, diseases, nuclear and biological threats, and environmental concerns as a reason for the establishment of a world government to take charge of these affairs, to solve the problems with modern science, and establish peace. It is the same argument that says poverty is why we have crime in our cities. All of these globalist solutions ignore the fundamental nature of man, which is fallen as Genesis declares [Gen. 3:15], and apart from a new birth as Jesus declared [Jn. 3], is under the influence of the evil one. All we lack at this time is some charismatic leader to step forward.

The so-called four horsemen of the apocalypse, as presented in Revelation chapter six, are very much in view in any last-days scenario. Certainly, the presence of war is preeminently in view at this time as we have seen in the previous chapter and in our news media. It is at this point we should look at the other factors exacerbating the end-times scenario. This chapter will briefly try to set the record straight on global trends in population, food, famine, health, and the ability of technology to solve our problems. Chapter eight will then deal with the political/religious scenario in what is believed to be the *Last Days* of this present dispensation.

A. Population Bomb

In 1968 the radical environmentalist Paul Ehrlich published the book *The Population Bomb*.[43] This book panicked the world with dire predictions of millions dying of starvation by the year 2000. It fomented population control and forced abortions in some of the most populous nations such as China. Planned Parenthood and the UN have gone into the education and abortion battle in a big way, with the result that some are even talking now about a population implosion.[44] But the truth is, there is a steady growth in the world population which will in the future give us some of the events seen in the last days in the book of the Revelation.

Since 1930, the year my life began, the population of the world has tripled, going from two billion to six billion in the year 1999. It is predicted to double again, i.e. twelve billion, by the year 2015. The following table shows the exponential growth in world population:

Year	People living in the World
2350 B.C.	8
1 A.D.	200,000,000
1804 A.D.	1,000,000,000
1927 A.D.	2.000,000,000
1974 A.D.	4,000,000,000
1999 A.D.	6,000,000,000

These data are consistent with all the known written and scientific records. It should be noted that these data are entirely consistent with the biblical flood epoch with just eight souls surviving just some 4350 years ago. If an evolutionary time scale is to be considered, where are the records, either written or in the fossils, or living today of the 3,000,000,000,000 souls who should have walked the earth in that scenario?

The average number of births per woman in the year 2000 was published by the web page www.overpopulation.org as 1.6 in developed countries, 3.0 in less developed countries, and 5.1 in the least developed countries. China is an anomaly in this statistic with its 1.26 billion people holding to a 1.07 percent growth rate due to compulsory birth control policies.

While the population growth presents some significant hunger problems to the world, they are all primarily sociopolitical, and the Western nations are capable of producing enough food to feed the problem areas at least through the year 2015. The population bomb also is producing some significant refugee and homeland-seeking problems for large groups of people. These problems have produced a cultural diversity in the United States that made it difficult to deal with 9–11 in several areas.

B. Water

The ancient mariner said, "Water, water everywhere and not a drop to drink." The report *Global 2000* predicted serious water shortages would produce drought, famine, and conflict in various parts of the world by the year 2000. The crisis turned out to be not as acute as forecast, but it is still there and becoming more acute as *Global Trends 2015*[45] predicts. Many of the water problems can be solved by technology, e.g. desalination of sea water, and deep wells with wind mill pumps etc., but there must be a time of peace and it will be costly.

C. Food

The global studies titled Global 2000 and Global 2015 estimated shortages would become critical in many areas with serious famine by the year 2015, but the US and Canada can, with current production capability, feed a population of twelve billion with wheat, corn and soybeans. The major deterrents to this happening are social, political, and religious. Typical of this evil were the days in the 1970s when the United States sent several large merchant ships full of grain to alleviate the need in flood-ravaged Bangladesh; it rotted in the harbors while the political factions fought over who would distribute it and get the credit and profit from it.

D. Energy

Energy, which fuels the industrial nations' lifestyle, is abundant in the world in the form of both replaceable and non-replaceable forms. But its use, availability etc. is so tied up in the social and political struggles of fallen mankind that major conflicts are forecast. The modern Western and advanced Asian countries such as Japan and now China, use a disproportionate amount of the non-renewable energy on the planet. The United States has approximately three percent of the world's proven petroleum reserves. The total proven reserves for the unstable Middle East is 64.5 percent. In 2002, the US consumed more than 25% of total world production, about half of it in gasoline. Some 25% of our imported petroleum, and the US imports more than 50% of what is used, comes from the Middle East. These nations, i.e. the modern Western and Asian countries, also have the technology to solve most of our problems. Through increased efficiency and renewable sources they can meet the world's needs well into this next century. Energy has an impact and even can provide solutions in the food, water, and environment areas. There is abundant energy to meet the world's basic needs, but the cost and distribution is unacceptable to many nations. More than half of America's electricity comes from coal (46). Coal is an abundant source of energy, which has been used for centuries, and could supply the free world's demand for energy for the next century. The environmentalists would like to remove it because it is said to produce smog, acid rain, and climate change. The Department of Energy has said that the Zero Emission Coal Alliance (ZECA) has designed a zero emission coal plant. It remains to be seen who will win this battle.

There are many well-documented studies of the world's energy problems, which could be cited in this section, but every one has some ax to grind regarding the sociopolitical/economic environment being pushed in the study. *Global Trends 2015* was an example of this, and while it tried to be predictive of the most realistic appraisal, it seems that every scenario presented goes up in smoke in light of 9–11. *War* is the most likely result of many of these scenarios.

E. Environment

No doubt about it, the environment is going downhill, as the needs of a burgeoning population make more and more demands on a post-flood environment of increasing deserts, glacial effects, and the ubiquitous second law of thermodynamics. A recent study of the glaciers on Mt. Kilimanjaro showed an eighty percent reduction in the snowcap from 1890 to 1990 (NOVA, Nov. 2003). It is estimated that the ice will be completely gone by 2015. Global warming, which has been going on since Noah's days, is very evident in the major glaciated areas of the world. To blame this on modern man and his machines does not hold true to the magnitude of the problem and the scientific evidence.

The evolution from fire to fossil fuels to nuclear energy is a path of improved human health and welfare arising from technological advances by a creative and industrious world of people created in the image of God. The debate over global warming, as exemplified by the Kyoto Protocol,[47] has ignored the fact that much of the world, such as China, India, and Africa are still a century behind and are too poor or too warlike to implement the environmental solutions available through technology and a caring government. For most of the evil world under false religious leaderships such as communism, Hinduism, Buddhism, and Islam, the worst environmental scenarios are being written today. Ecology and peace will become the unifying call to all religions, as they will be called together in a satanic/pagan spirituality to rescue the planet. Much of this will be done under the guise of evolutionary science; globalists and environmentalists will continue to use scare tactics to win support for their causes, even though it is a well-documented fact that ninety-six percent of all greenhouse gas emissions occur naturally.[46] Solar activity, volcanoes, and lightning-started forest fires dwarf any human-induced effect on global warming. The wealthy countries can and have cleaned up the air and water environment, but we must not let the extremists in the Planetary Society, Greenpeace or any other satanically deluded group control the determined course for this nation under God.

F. Health

Worldwide health crises seem to be cropping up, especially in the third world. AIDS has reached epidemic proportion in Africa; it is said that six percent of the Russian army also has it (re. *Avoiding Armageddon*, PBS, April 2003). Other diseases such as smallpox, avian flu, and one called SARS, are on the rise. The question is: will the World Health Organization (WHO) be able to cope with these global pestilences?

G. Secular Humanism and Naturalism

One of the best-organized attacks upon biblical revelation and morality is a tool of Satan called secular humanism. This movement, promoted by a group known as the American Humanist Association, has permeated our American society with its *Humanist Manifesto I* in 1933, and *Humanist Manifesto II* in 1973. These documents, signed by a small number of influential people holding significant power in many areas of society, were an effort to throw God out of the areas of science, the arts, literature, the media, philosophy, education, and politics. One of the doctrinal pillars of the *Humanist Manifesto II* is, "No deity will save us; we must save ourselves."[48] By reading through these documents you will see a well-organized attack on the Bible and the very concept of God, which is called "the highest form of self deception" which the world would be better off without. These people drive the environmentalist movement, and the teaching of *evolution*, and have become the high priests of many of the so-called advanced civilizations. The teaching of evolution, which is inherent in naturalism's view of the world, has been said to be the dominant dogma of the Western world. Proposing that this teaching is scientific and not religious, and thus intellectually superior, naturalism stands in opposition and at *war* with the faith-based and historically accurate, worldview of Christianity.

Evolutionists spoken of by Peter in the last days (2 Pet. 3) are willingly ignorant of the evidence for the Genesis Flood which was God's previous judgment of a warring world. These secular humanists, evolutionists, naturalists have dominated the fields of science and their educators are propagating a philosophy and culture that deny the reality or the necessity of the coming judgment. This philosophy has been a war-inducing survival-of-the-fittest struggle as Hitler, Mao, and Stalin, all advocated evolution. Viktor Frankl, a survivor of the Holocaust, wrote that: "The gas chambers of Auschwitz were the ultimate consequence of the theory that man is nothing but the product of heredity and environment, or as the Nazis liked to say, blood and soil. I am absolutely convinced that the gas chambers of Auschwitz, Treblinka, and Maidanek were ultimately prepared not in some ministry or other in Berlin, but rather at the desks and in the lecture halls of nihilistic scientists and philosophers."[62] Many thousands of Hitler's henchmen were involved in the mass exterminations; millions of ordinary Germans were seduced by evolution-based propaganda films into accepting the elimination of the mentally handicapped and incurably ill as normal. This doctrine was applied to the Jews as well as the pre-war Nazi racial-hygiene programs and became the precursors to the Holocaust. This doctrine was praised by many leading American scientists as scientifically enlightened.

In addition, the environmentalists, most of whom are evolutionists, are trying to preserve a lost and dying world with their priority on the environment rather than on the redemption of mankind where God has placed it. Nothing is more enlightening than the United Nations' agenda as presented at the Millennium Summit in September 2000. The whole presentation was meant to strengthen the role of the world body, (the UN) in the new world order. Their goals were listed as: freedom from fear and wars; globalization and governance; sustaining our planet for future generations (climate change, water crisis, bio-diversity, and conservation which is the environmentalists' agenda to the letter); and freedom from want—citing poverty, education, health, HIV/AIDS, slums etc. as problems only the United Nations can deal with effectively. Is there any question that there will be many advocates for this approach among the free nations; Scripture tells us there will be war in the last days, not peace.

Just where all of this will lead is the subject of the following chapter. It is believed that the conclusions of *Global Trends 2015* are seriously flawed in light of 9–11 and the current position of Islam among the many nations. It appears that we have entered the *last days of the longest war* and it is doubtful that a time of true peace will be implemented based on globalization. Nations no longer will hold sway as civilizations will transcend nations and Samuel Huntington will be proven a prophet. The reasons for this position are answered in the following chapter by the Scripture that the Creator gave us.

CHAPTER 8

A Biblical Look at the Last Days of the Longest War

THE MARCH TOWARD ARMAGEDDON

We fight in honorable fashion for the good of mankind; fearless of the future; unheeding of our individual fates; with unflinching hearts and undimmed eyes; we stand at Armageddon, and we battle for the Lord!

—Theodore Roosevelt, June 1912

A nationally syndicated columnist recently described President Bush's Middle East positions as *Armageddon on the Potomac*. As we see from the statement of Teddy Roosevelt, it is not the first time that an apocalyptic worldview held the attitude of a president. When the political system gives us godly leaders, they will not be unaware of the biblical scenario of the last days of this age.

The events of recent days, such as the 9–11 strike, the war in Afghanistan, Iraq, and Israel, the Muslim nation's evil empire, the threat of wars around the globe, etc., should impel all Bible students to make a fresh study of biblical prophecy. It would be of interest to see where some of the current events and Bible prophecies line up time wise; an exercise which is not against the will of God as Peter declared in 1 Peter 1:10–11.

At this time the world is setting up for the following scenario as the Islamic nations are polarized against Israel and the USA. Currently, the Western nations under President Bush's leadership will try to divide Islam, by trying to philosophically separate the terrorists from the non-militant Islamic people. But in the end we will see that pure Islam **is** the militant Islam whose mission is subjection, not peace. As of publication date it appears that in the coming days, Afghanistan will be permanently set free from the Taliban and Osama Bin-Laden, and Saddam and Arafat will be annihilated in the war against terror but the terrorism will not go away. We are and have been at war with Islam for some time with 9–11 being the definitive turning point, which as a free nation we can no longer stand quietly still. This author believes that President Bush was correct to preemptively go after Islamic leaders who harbor terrorists, and while he is unable to say that we are at war with Muslims, it is clear that the Muslim world has declared a jihad, a holy war, against the United States and Israel. According to the Israeli *GAMLA.org* website this preemptive strike approach is now an official policy of Israel regarding any Islamic nation with weapons of mass destruction, especially chemical and biological, as of May 17th 2004.

Regarding the Arab, in Genesis 16:11–16, the angel of the LORD (i.e. Christ) said that Ishmael would be "a wild ass of a man; and his hand would be against every man, and every man's hand against him; and he shall dwell before the face of all his brethren." Ishmael is the father of the Arabs and the progenitor of Mohammed, the false prophet of Islam who spoke of an appearance of the angel of the Lord to justify his proclamations. Those who are satanically inspired, characteristically claim this authority. Salmon Rushdie got it right when he referred to parts of the Koran as the "Satanic Verses." This does not mean that all Arabs, who make up only thirty-seven percent of the Muslim world, are satanically led. With the Arabs, just as with every other nation (Greek: *ethnos*), there are the children of God called out (Rev. 7:9–17). This vision of the apostle John in Revelation chapter seven is particularly applicable to this time as this author believes we have entered the last days covered in chapters 4–19.

It should also be noted that Joseph Smith, the false prophet of Mormonism, like Mohammed, counterfeited the appearance of a manifestation of God. Joseph Smith said he saw, in three contradictory statements: an angel, the Son of God, the Father and the Son, in his falsification of his authority.[49] While it is possible that both Mohammed and Joseph Smith were visited by a satanic emissary as evidenced by the fruit of their followers, this is just one more confirmation of the long war against the true seed. It should be noted here regarding Mormonism that Jon Krakauer, in his book titled *Under the Banner of Heaven*, calls the Mormon Church "a major world religion, the first such faith to emerge since Islam." With eleven million members, the Mormons could easily lead the movement to back the antichrist when he makes himself known to the Western world.

With the current state of affairs we could expect to see some major fighting with the more extreme Muslim nations and the U.S. allied with Great Britain, and Israel. The Scripture foresees a temporary peace in the Middle East, probably spearheaded by the U.N. with the European Union in tow, then as forecast in Daniel 9, Matt. 24, 2 Thessalonians 2, the final **Last Days** scenario. It is in this scenario that the Jews will then build the temple under the protection of a coalition of liberal nations. That the Jews plan to build such a temple is as sure as the latest news from Jerusalem on Friday, April 5, 2002 when Rabbis Makover and Richman of the Temple

Institute certified a red heifer born in Israel as a candidate for the purification of the temple[50] as described in the Torah (Num. 19). Fundamental Islam will eventually get riled up by their imams to invade Israel. Jerusalem has become the burdenstone of all nations as God said it would (Zech. 12:3). All major nations will be involved in this scenario as they approach the time of Jacob's trouble i.e. the last three-and-one-half years called the great Tribulation (Dan. 12; Matt. 24; Rev. 7:14, and other related Scriptures). Of course God's Word also promises eventual deliverance to the remnant inhabitants of Jerusalem and the reign of His Son on David's throne (Zech. 12:7–9; 14:1–21). This will be dealt with in chapter 9.

Predominant Dispensational View of the Seven-year Tribulation

Dr. Renald Showers, noted author and teacher with the Friends of Israel ministry, paints the following picture of the last days which he allocates to a seven-year period of tribulation:

> Daniel 11:40 declares, "At the time of the end the king of the South shall attack him, and the king of the North shall come against him." Dr. Showers understands this to predict that during the first half of the Tribulation, Egypt (the king of the south) and Syria (the king of the north) will move against Israel. The Revived Roman Empire, which is the protector of Israel (Dan. 9:27), i.e. the Western world powers, soon to be led by the one who is the antichrist, will invade and conquer Syria and Lebanon, then quickly move through the glorious land (Israel: Dan. 11:41) and go on to conquer Egypt (Dan. 11:42–43). It will look as if the entire Middle East is about to come under his domination. This, of course, would mean that he controls much of the world's oil reserves as well.

This brings about the next invasion of the Middle East by a massive military force from Iran (Persia), Sudan (Ethiopia), Libya (Put), Turkey (Gomer and Togarmah), and Russia (Gog, the land of Magog) (Ezek. 38:2–6). This force will come against Antichrist's ally Israel (Ezek. 38:8–16; Dan. 11:44a). In response to this invasion against Israel, Antichrist will rush to protect the land of Israel with the goal of destroying this multi-national force (Dan. 11:44b). But before the antichrist gets there, God intervenes supernaturally to destroy the armed forces of Gog et al. in the mountains of Israel (Ezek. 38:14–39:6). As a result, Antichrist will have a free hand to do what he wants in the Middle East. He will decide to make Jerusalem the capital of what he hopes will become his worldwide empire (Dan. 11:45a). At this point, which Dr. Showers calls the middle of the seven-year tribulation, the antichrist will put a stop to the re-instituted sacrifices of the Jews in their new temple (Dan. 9:27b), take his seat in that temple and make the blasphemous claim that he is God (2 Thess. 2:3–4; Dan. 7:8, 20, 25a, 11:36–37; Rev. 13:5–6). He will begin to desolate Israel (Dan. 9:27c; Matt. 24:15–21) and wage war against the tribulation saints (Rev. 13:7).

The third invasion against Israel will involve the political rulers and armies of all the nations of the world (Joel 3:1–2, 9–16; Zeph. 3:8, 12–14; Rev. 16:12–16, 19). They will begin to gather against Israel at the end of the seven-year period when the sixth judgment bowl is unleashed (Rev. 16:12–16). Two-thirds of the Jews in the land will perish and only one third will be left when the true Messiah Jesus returns in His second coming. The one-third remnant of Jews will repent when they see Him (Zech. 12:10ff). God will cleanse them of their sin (Zech. 13:1). Then Jesus will wage war against the armies of Satan arrayed against Israel. This is *Armageddon*! Then He will establish the millennial kingdom (Zech. 12–14; Rev. 19:11–20:6). See end notes.[51, 52]

Commentary on Last Days

Thus, Dr. Showers has given the predominant dispensational view of the biblical prophecies concerning the last days of this dispensation. It appears that all the major players in the last days are now in position, and we who are believers are eagerly anticipating the return of Jesus the Messiah to take His people to meet Him in the air (1 Thess. 4:13–18). The term *Messiah* comes from the Hebrew Scriptures and refers to the expected king and deliverer of the Jews (Dan. 9:25) of whom Andrew, Simon Peter's brother, said of Jesus, "We have found the Messiah" (Jn. 1:41). This is not the only view held by various religious leaders. The Jews to this day are still looking for their Messiah; and every Passover they set a place at their Passover meal for Elijah who is to come as His forerunner. The Arab world likewise holds that the messiah, or *mahdi* in the Islamic version, is on the doorstep to sally forth from his heavenly hiding place to usher in a new Islamic dominion over all the world. On a new internet site called *Armageddon*, the following detailed timetable is offered for this event:

"First Fahd, the ailing 81-year-old king of Saudi Arabia, will die. After that, the mahdi will appear, and his rule will spread quickly over the Arabian peninsula, Iran and across to Jerusalem. At this point the Muslim invasion into Russia, China, and India will begin. Turkey and Italy will be conquered immediately afterwards, then a false messiah will appear, and be eliminated by Jesus, (Islam recognizes Jesus as one of the prophets who preceded Mohammed)." Several Islamic writers, such as Haran Yahu of Turkey, have said Jesus will then acknowledge Islam and Allah as the one true God, and all the nations will be subjected to Islamic rule. Even the Jews are aware of this teaching, as seen in a recent article by Ehud Ya'ari in *The Jerusalem Report,* March 24, 2003. It appears that President Bush has put a serious roadblock in the way of this prediction.

The Bible does give the prophecy that a charismatic leader will appear on the scene in the last days who will fulfill the prophecies of Matthew 24 and 2 Thessalonians 2 as an abomination to God. David Brickner, executive director of Jews for Jesus, believes the current struggle in the Middle East is the conflict of the ages that will usher in the antichrist. He points out that the antichrist will have to be a Muslim, to enable a Jewish temple to be built on the temple mount. There are several scenarios in which this would fit into the biblical prophecies, but enough has been covered already to see that we are in the *last days of the longest war.*

It is clear that we are living in a very dynamic time with the scene changing almost daily. While the Jewish hope, which is blind to the truth for a time (see Romans chapter 11) will be solved when Christ returns and they look upon whom they have pierced (Zech. 12:10), then the world in general will realize that the Islamic lie is of the devil.

It must be admitted that there are many questions with Dr. Showers' scenario. Not only with the description of the various events, but with the sequence, and the obvious omission of the scenes and signs recorded in Matthew 24 and Rev 8–16. The world-encompassing natural disasters of asteroids (Rev. 8:10–11), eclipses (Rev. 8:12), famine, earthquakes, the death of all living things in the sea (Rev. 16:3) etc. which are an important aspect of the last three-and-a-half years of the Tribulation, will go well beyond the scenes focused on Israel. To many in the world these aspects will be more important than those listed in Dr. Showers' scenario which deals primarily with the Middle East.

The events Dr. Showers lists as coming at the mid-point in the Tribulation all come out of the Ezekiel prophecy in chapters 38 and 39, but this prophecy is most probably tied to the final rebellion after the millennium as spelled out in Revelation 20:7–10. Ezekiel 37:15–28 speaks of a time of peace that precedes the time of Ezekiel 38 and 39. This time is one where "David my servant is king over them" (Ezek. 37:24), which can only be the millennial age of Revelation 20. Thus the time of Gog and Magog, both specifically mentioned, (Ezek. 38:2 and Rev. 20:8), fit perfectly with the final rebellion, and not the seven-year tribulation which precedes the millennial kingdom. Furthermore, Ezekiel chapter 40 and following speaks of that new city which ties to the New Jerusalem of Revelation 21 and 22, which will be dealt with in depth in the following chapter.

About all that can really be said about all of these scenarios is that most of the actors in them can be said to be on the scene today, and therefore it is concluded that we are in the *Last Days*. Psalm 83 gives significant insight into these nations. Not only does Psalm 83 name the nations which are currently allied under Islamic Jihad, verses 5–8, but the Scripture states exactly what they would be saying: "Come and let us cut them off from being a nation, that the name of Israel may be remembered no more" (v. 4). With the nation of Israel returned to the land promised to them by God, we see not only the nations aligned under the satanic banner of Islam, but others under the atheistic banner of communism ready to destroy Israel. With others under a pseudo secular/religious banner of the Western world of Roman heritage it is appropriate to see the scene as Daniel saw in his prophecies. The Christian should not despair over the world crisis, for this is not the best world, but in God's eyes it is the best path to the best world as Israel's King David understood (2 Sam. 22:31a, Ps. 18:30a).

It is Zechariah to whom we might look to be the real key to the events of these days. First of all, Matthew writes that it was Zechariah's prophecy that Jesus fulfilled when He entered Jerusalem on that first day of the week in the thirty-third year of His life (Matt. 21:1–9; Zech. 9:9). There were three other prophecies in Zechariah, which were fulfilled at His first coming, so with this proof of inspiration, it should be Zechariah that we should look to when He returns again. Consider the following prophetic utterances of Zechariah concerning the events of the last days: 1. The regathering of an as-yet unbelieving nation of Israel which we see as accomplished (Zech. 10:9–12); 2. The world against Jerusalem and the present state of affairs, where Jerusalem is a "cup of trembling" and a "burdenstone for all peoples" (Zech. 12: 2, 3); 3. The near future when the Jews will recognize that the crucified One was their messiah and one-third of the nation will believe and be delivered (Zech. 12:7–13:9); 4. The triumphant return of Christ to the Mount of Olives (Zech. 14: 1–8), and the millennial kingdom which will be set up on earth (Zech. 14: 9–21). Are we not almost there?

There is one prophesied event that will occur in the last days, which deserves a special comment. This event is the so-called Rapture of Christ's church. The surety of this event is proclaimed by Jesus in Matthew 24 and 25, and testified to by Paul in 1 Corinthians 15, and First and Second Thessalonians, and by John in Revelation 3:10, and chapter 7. This event is as sure as the Resurrection, and the Ascension into heaven (see Acts chapter one). It will be unmistakable as the signs in the heavens and the trumpet will declare, so Jesus says not to go looking for a false return by a false messiah (Matt. 24:23–27). I am not prepared at this time to dogmatically—nor is anyone I know able to—detail the events of the last days. Biblical prophecy often looks proleptically as Zechariah does, i.e. across the peaks of the coming events, and until they happen few can fill in the blanks. For example, the two comings of the Messiah was a mystery to many such as in the Essene community at the time of Christ. The historical record of the Essenes records that until the unveiling of the coming of God's Son, and the revealing of the New Testament, they held the view that there must be two Messiahs, one who was a suffering servant from Isaiah 53, and one who was the son of David, a conquering king to deliver Israel. It may be that there are *two* raptures. The first one of the church, just prior to the abomination of Matthew 24 and 2 Thessalonians 2, and the second one of the tribulation saints just prior to the seventh trumpet of Revelation 7 and 11. Or it may be that there is only one. That it will come is without question as Jesus taught and Paul wrote (Matt. 24 and 25; Jn. 14: 1–6; 1 Cor. 15; 1 and 2 Thess; Rev. 7 and 11).

Some of the pertinent prophecies to the time of this end are the writings of Hosea who declared how long the Jews would be without a king, prince, or sacrificial system (Hos. 3:4, 6:2). Of course, the sacrificial system ended with the death of Christ as the temple veil was rent in A.D. 32, and will not resume until the temple is rebuilt in the last days. If this is exactly 2000 years (Hosea's two days of chapter 3 is understood as 2000 years from chapter 6), we may be looking at the year A.D. 2032 for the end of the age. It is more likely that the time line from the end of Judaic *salvation* as described in Hebrews chapter 11 to the end of the times of the Gentiles—the church—begins with the coming of the Holy Spirit at Pentecost in A.D. 32 (Acts 2) and ends with His return for the church to meet Him in the air (1 Thess. 4:18).

The pre-Christian Jewish scholars, writers of the Talmud and the Mishnah, as well as the writings of the entire early church, stated that there would be six millennia of man from the creation to the seventh millennium when the King of kings will reign in

Jerusalem.[53] As this monograph has shown, we are demonstrably at the end of the sixth millennium since the creation. Finally, the Scripture tells us there would be a severe time of trouble for the nation of Israel when the archangel Michael would stand aside and allow the great Tribulation to take place before the deliverance of God's people (Dan. 12:1). Moreover, this time is characterized by a time of unprecedented travel and increase in knowledge (Dan. 12:4). A recent estimate from the SMU School of Engineering stated that "Forty years ago, the world's body of knowledge doubled every 15 years. Today [April 2004], it is doubling every three years. By some estimates, 10 years from now, when today's students are graduated and in the job market, knowledge will be doubling every 12 to 14 months." If the prophet Daniel didn't describe the current the space age, global satellite hookups, the internet, and the information age, I don't know how better to describe it. It could be that this time started with the beginning of the seventh millennium and the Al-Aqsa Jihad which started on New Year's Day (Rosh Ha Shannah) 28 September 2000 A.D. Since the mid-tribulation point of 2 Thessalonians has not appeared in the spring of 2004 it can be assumed that the date of 28 Sept. 2000 was not the start of the seven year tribulation. The Al-Aqsa Jihad has been said by several Arab leaders, including Arafat, to be the final Jihad which will not end until Israel is no more! This means we cannot expect peace to come until the Western world can subdue Islam, most probably under a UN banner, having been united by a charismatic leader who turns out to be the antichrist who will fulfill the abomination Christ spoke of (Matt. 24) and Paul wrote of in 2 Thessalonians 2.

Some thoughts on the European Union and the Bible are in order at this point. Rob Congden, a Friends of Israel teacher in Scotland, has presented a cogent study on how the EU is trying to fulfill the centuries-long effort to unify Europe.[54] From the days of

Constantine down through Charlemagne, Napoleon, up through the Third Reich of Adolph Hitler, the dream was fostered in a pseudo-Christian anti-Semitic scenario that may yet fit the biblical scene given in Daniel 7:23–25. Where do the ten nations come from when the present EU consists of fifteen or more? It could come from a restructuring in the nations as Hitler had planned.[55] It was Hitler's post-war plan that conceived of a ten-region set up under his ultimate authority that would rule Europe for 1000 years—the Third Reich. The European unification dream not only existed in the mind of Hitler, but in the French from the days of Napoleon to the time of de Gaulle who, in the early days after World War II, wanted "a Europe of the fatherlands from the Atlantic to the Urals."[55]

The present war with the more evil aspects of Islam in Israel, Afghanistan, Iraq etc. will certainly accelerate the advents of these prophesied events. Certainly we Americans have the right to deal with terrorist-supporting regimes, as our president and this writer understands. The opportunity of the antichrist to come to power may well be that he will provide a solution to peace in the Middle East, possibly through the European Union's efforts of which he will be proclaimed head. This period of peace will prove to be temporal as Daniel the prophet tells us (Dan. 9), and will only last three-and-one-half years prior to the antichrist ushering in the last three-and-one-half years of great Tribulation such as the world has never seen before (Matt. 24; Rev. 9–19).

So we may rightly ask, what time is it? It may well be that this last days scenario is not as speculated, but we have seen from the previous chapter that we are at best only twelve years away from a scenario where both the scientific scenarios of chapter seven, and the biblical scenarios of this chapter, will become synergistic and supercritical. We *are* in the *last days of the long war against God*, and we need to be strong, endure the hardship, share the truth contained in this book, and look to the promised future.

Of certain interest is the history and fall of Babylon as presented in the book of the Revelation chapters 14 through 19. Revelation 14:8 declares, "Babylon the great has fallen." Today, history has returned to the land of the Tigris and Euphrates, ancient Babylon, the cradle of civilization. The pre-flood Eden was in this area (Gen. 2:10–14). The fall of mankind to the lies of Satan happened here (Gen. 3:15). The post-Flood events at Babel occurred here, from which Babylon gets its name. The names for this area in the Bible are Babylon, Land of Shinar, and Mesopotamia (land between the rivers). This land, known today as Iraq, has given rise to some of the world's most brutal tyrants: from Nimrod of Nineveh c. 2100 B.C., and his descendants the Assyrians under Sargon who in three campaigns from 720 to 711 B.C. turned the northern kingdom of Israel into a vassal state, to the Babylonians of Nebuchadnezzar who took the southern kingdom of Judah into captivity in three campaigns from 606 to 586 B.C, all the way down to Saddam Hussein. This land also gave birth to the one whom the Jews call Father Abraham, who was called out of Ur, which is not far from the city of Basra. The ancient city of Babylon, which Saddam had been restoring, is about twenty-five miles south of Baghdad.

The prophet Jeremiah foretold the demise of Nebuchadnezzar's Babylon at the hands of the Medes 539 B.C. (Jer. 50:1–51:16). The city has been little more than an ancient archaeological site until Iraq and Saddam revived it in this past century. For the past two decades Iraq has been the focus of worldwide strife and three major wars. Now, in these last days, America has realized her duty to freedom and liberty and done something about this evil empire. Indelibly burned in the mind of every world culture is the fall of Baghdad as seen on television in 2003. Could it be that this was the fulfillment of the biblical prophecy of Revelation 14:8? Consider the following: 1. The Scripture indicates that all nations drank of her wine (Rev. 14:8). Could this be that the world as a whole was involved in the oil riches or in her idolatry with Islam, which today seems to be seeping into every corner of the world? 2. Revelation 17:1 through 19:10 speaks of religious fornication. Islam leads the world in pursuit of a false religion. It is stated that Babylon is drunk with the blood of the saints. There has been from this land of Babylon a vast history of killing the saints. Beginning on the plains of Shinar through Nimrod (Gen. 10:9–10, 11:1–9) down through the ages, continuing with the Islamic conquering of Northern Africa in the eighth century A.D. and into our present era with 9–11 and the continuing terror around the world. This evil system will reach its pinnacle just before the Second Advent. Today, Islam is killing the saints in many areas of the world as discussed in earlier chapters. The woman of Revelation 17 is a religious system connected to the past, present, and future and finally to Babylon on the Euphrates. Revelation 18:3 reiterates that the kings of the earth have all drunk with her and become rich. It has been shown that France, Russia, China, et al. had billions tied up in Saddam's regime. It is interesting that ships, i.e. oil tankers, were fundamental to her wealth. So now we see the fall of Babylon, and all the world has watched it on global television networks just as Revelation 18:15–18 mentions.

Some Bible teachers have proposed that the prophecy of Isaiah 19:23–25 is in the process of being fulfilled as highways are being built from Assyria through Israel to Egypt. However, this prophecy is rightly understood as the blessing of Assyria, Egypt, and Israel "in that day" i.e. that day when the LORD of hosts reigns in Jerusalem. This is during the millennial age and fits perfectly in what the nations are doing in Zechariah 14 as they travel to Jerusalem to worship the King, the LORD Jesus.

So the question remains, what time is it? We have seen that many events are synergistically falling into place that say it is very close to the end of this age. This writer cannot be dogmatic, as there are some prophetic events that have not been fulfilled in the fall of Babylon and the events in the Middle East. One of these is the drying up of the Euphrates as prophesied in Jeremiah 50:38 and Revelation 16:12, which is placed in the sixth bowl judgment, so it is assured that we are not in the last days of the Tribulation. Furthermore, there has not been any covenant of peace promised to Israel as predicted in Daniel 9:27 which must come before the mid-tribulation point; some say before the start of the seven years. If the UN signs a covenant to protect the state of Israel and gives the Palestinians a stake in the process, we can probably then say what time it is.

Often overlooked in the study of last days are the thirty-fourth and thirty-fifth chapters of Isaiah. In the thirty-fourth chapter, God deals with the climax and immediate aftermath of the great Tribulation, which deals with the day of the LORD's vengeance upon all nations (Isa. 34:2, 8). The thirty-fifth chapter of Isaiah reveals that after the desolation of the Tribulation, the earth's environment and its second law of thermodynics aspects will be restored to the antediluvian conditions. Jesus spoke of this time as the regeneration, but a careful rendering of the Greek here translates the word *palingenesis* as *again genesis* (Matt. 19:28). So, in some measure, the conditions of Genesis 1 will prevail during the coming millennial kingdom age. Which brings us to the following chapter, which speaks of our certain future hope.

New Jerusalem the Eternal City of God

CHAPTER 9

Beyond the War—
The Certain Future

This is not the best world. But it is the best path to the best world.

—Anon

This world is not falling apart, it is falling in place.

—Anne Graham Lotz

When the last days of this age are consummated and the Lord Jesus Christ has returned to reign on earth, the Scripture declares that, "The kingdom of this world is become the kingdom of our Lord, and of His Christ, and he shall reign into the ages and the ages" (Rev. 11:15). The Greek *eis tous aiwvas twv aiwvwv* is usually translated *forever and ever*, but I have chosen a more literal rendering to see that there are two ages revealed, both here and in the last three chapters of the Revelation, namely the thousand years on this earth, and the eternal state throughout eternity in the new heaven and earth. This chapter will attempt to explain what the Scripture reveals. Our future hope is based on biblical prophecy, and we who have believed in Jesus as our Lord and our God (Jn. 20:28–31) can expect the following:

The Millennial Reign of Christ

Purpose of the Millennial Kingdom

This 1000 year period reflects a fulfillment of the prophecies in which God is glorified primarily through the establishment of a theocratic kingdom centered in Israel which God calls His Glory. God's relation to Israel is permanent (Deut. 4:37, 7:8) as Moses said to God, recalling the promises given in Genesis: "Remember Abraham, Isaac, and Israel, Your servants, to whom You swore by Your own self, and said to them, 'I will multiply your descendants as the stars of heaven; and all this land that I have spoken of I give to your descendants, and they shall inherit it forever'" (Ex. 32:13). Thus, we look for God to restore the land to Israel in the last days. This Kingdom period is when Jesus the Messiah will reign in Jerusalem (Ezek. 34; Zech. 14; Matt. 24; Rev. 20), fulfilling God's promises to Abraham, Israel, and David (Isa. 24:23). Furthermore, the millennial age marks a return to Genesis 1, where God had given man the rule over the earth which man deeded to Satan at the Fall. This is clearly understood when we read that Satan offered Jesus the rule which Satan said had been delivered to him (Luke 4:6). But the second Adam, Jesus, defeated Satan at the cross and He will rightfully rule this kingdom (Rom. 5 and Rev. 20).

This Sabbath millennium—the millennial kingdom is said not to be literal by many in the church in spite of the clear statements of Revelation chapter 20 and the often-overlooked revelation of Hebrews 4:3–11. This blindness and confusion is the product of both ignorance and so-called covenant theology or replacement theology that has generally rejected Israel in eschatology in favor of a supplanting church which inherits all of the promises. The extreme manifestation of this shows up in the British Israelite traditions which state that the British are descendants of the lost tribes of Israel and in Christ have supplanted Israel, receiving all of the promises—nonsense that was readily incorporated into the false prophecies of the Mormon leader Joseph Smith in the 1800s.

This dispensation, the millennial kingdom, is a time when Satan is bound, yet mankind, the portion which are still in the flesh, will still have to choose whether to be a child of the King. This is the last of the testing dispensations. This kingdom is centered in Jerusalem with Jesus the Messiah (Hebrew: Yeshua *HaMashiach*) ruling in David's seat with the faithful of Israel, while the faithful believers of the time from Adam to Abraham and the Gentile church are spread throughout the world administering the kingdom as resurrected saints. It is the fulfillment of all the Old and New Testament promises for a kingdom to Israel, as expected by the apostles (Acts 1:6). Just exactly what the saints will be doing as they live and reign with Christ (Rev. 20:6) can only be guessed at. John would understand that the nation of Israel would have the priestly role to be administering the offerings, and worship (Isa. 61:6; Zech. 8:20–23; Ex. 19:6), as well as controlling access to Christ and His judgments. Certainly, there will be many administrative responsibilities that will be given to the saints, as the people of the world will work and worship in the seventh millennium. Lifespan will be extended probably back to pre-Flood levels (Isaiah 65:18–25). This time, God will constitute a theocracy where Jesus, the last Adam (Rom. 5:12–21) will reign with His saints.

Physical Conditions in the Millennium

The passages in Isaiah chapters 11, 35, 51:3, and 65:20–25 all denote some reordering of the natural world, possibly a return to the Edenic state of Genesis chapter one as mentioned previously (Matt. 19:28). The configuration of the nation Israel at this time is described by Ezekiel as he lays out the land and the city with its millennial temple where the Messiah will be enthroned (Ezek. 40–47). There are some interesting passages, which relate to the environment and ecology in Isaiah and Ezekiel. Isaiah chapter 11 speaks of an animal kingdom without fear and predation which may be entirely consistent with Ezekiel 47:12 which speaks of an Edenic-like time when mankind returns to being a fruit-eating vegetarian as Genesis chapter one indicates.

But this is not the new heaven and new earth of the eternal state which is covered in the following section. It will be a joyous time when "the ransomed of the LORD shall return, and come to Zion with songs and everlasting joy upon their heads: they shall obtain joy and gladness, and sorrow and sighing shall flee away" (Isa. 35:10). This millennial kingdom is also part of the redemptive work of God. It is the answer to our prayer that Jesus taught us to say: "Thy kingdom come, Thy will be done, on earth as it is in heaven" (Lk. 11:2–4). It will also be a fulfillment of the many prophecies relating to a restored Israel with David's seed on the throne.

Inhabitants of the Millennial Kingdom

Resurrected: Old Testament saints—(Dan. 12:2, 13), and New Testament saints (1 Thess. 4:17–19; 2 Tim. 2:12; Rev. 7, 20:3–4). These saints are reigning over the millennial kingdom with Jesus the Christ, David's seed, as King in Jerusalem (Rev. 20:6). Every ruler is a resurrected saint and will be perfect in judgment and justice as they are now sinless and immortal.

Living remnant of the Tribulation—A saved remnant of the Jews, and a certain number of Gentiles (Zech. 12–14; Jer. 30:19, 20; Ezek. 47:22). These Gentiles are apparently the participants in the final rebellion or the *last war* after the millennial age when Satan is loosed for a little while (Rev. 20:7). There is a certain amount of mystery regarding this mix of resurrected and living inhabitants that has caused some of the covenant theologians to reject a millennial kingdom altogether. This is exacerbated by the sometimes proleptic nature of Old Testament prophecies which allow first and second comings of the Messiah, and the abomination spoken of by Daniel to have a 165 B.C. fulfillment and yet Jesus speaks of a second time (Matt. 24:15).

Time period

This Kingdom is for a period of one thousand years (Rev. 20: 1–10), immediately following the great tribulation (Rev. 4–19). This would perfectly fulfill the teaching of the Talmud, that there is to be a period of six millennia of man followed by a one millennium rule by the Messiah. It was reported by Justin Martyr that this is what the apostle John taught, and John, in his last days, wore a phylactery on his forehead that said "Holiness to the Lord" taken from Zech. 14:20 which describes the millennial age.

The Great White Throne Judgment

After the completion of the seventh millennium of man, the final rebellion of mankind occurs as Satan is released to claim his last subjects for his infernal kingdom, being made up of those who would not accept Jesus as Lord in the millennial age. The participants in this final rebellion are probably most tied to Ezekiel 38 and 39 and the nations of Gog and Magog (Rev. 20:8; Ezek. 38:2, 39:1, 6) which represent those who dwelt in the earth during the millennial kingdom and never came up to Jerusalem to pay homage to Christ (Zech. 14). This final rebellion is put down and the final judgment is set up. The Great White Throne is a judgment of those unbelievers who are judged according to their works, which implies levels of punishment in the lake of fire for all who obey not the gospel of Christ (2 Thess. 1:8).

The Scripture in several places indicates levels of punishment, as Jesus Himself said (Matt. 23:14). It should be noted that there is also a judgment of believers, although not at the Great White Throne event, since this is a judgment separating the people who are not in the Lamb's Book of Life. The judgment for believers is normally understood to be at the bema seat of Christ at a prior time (2 Cor. 5:10), i.e. prior to the assignment of ruling positions in the kingdom with levels of rewards and position for those who are in the Lamb's book of life (Rev. 20:15, 1 Cor. 3:11–15). It is conceivable that it is at the end of all judgments that the prophecy of 2 Peter 3:10 will be fulfilled, bringing an end to this fallen and condemned world, thereby paving the way for the new heavens and earth which are to follow.

The Eternal Kingdom

The New Jerusalem, the Eternal City

Our Creator has not left us in the dark regarding the final question that every man asks in this life, i.e. What is my hope after death? The Bible is full of God's promises of eternal life. Most notable is the promise Jesus gave us on the night before He was crucified when He said: "In my Father's house are many mansions: If it were not so, I would have told you. I go to prepare a place for you" (Jn. 14:2). It is evident that if eternal life, which is promised to all who believe on the Lord Jesus the Christ (Jn. 3:16), and this place, is to be all that it should be, it must be in an environment, which is radically better than this present one. In short we need a whole new creation, that is to say, a new heaven and a new earth. This is precisely what God has promised in His message to the apostle John as recorded in the book of the Revelation Chapter 21 and 22. This is the city which all of God's seed have looked for from the time of Genesis on to the present. Hebrews 11:10 states that the Old Testament believers "looked for a city which has foundations whose builder and maker is God." This did not change with the appearing of God's Son on this sin-cursed planet, and the writer of Hebrews says that today for the believer "here we have no continuing city, but we seek one to come" (Heb. 13:14).

Let us study our way through these two chapters. The apostle John writes: "And I saw a new heaven and a new earth, for the first heaven and the first earth had passed away. Also there was no more sea. Then I John, saw the holy city, New Jerusalem, coming down out of heaven from God, prepared as a bride adorned for her husband. And I heard a loud voice from heaven saying, "Behold, the tabernacle of God is with men, and He will dwell with them, and they shall be His people, and God Himself will be with them and be their God. And God will wipe away every tear from their eyes; there shall be no more death, nor sorrow, nor crying; and there shall be no more pain, for the former things have passed away" (Rev. 21:1–4). Thus, we see this new heaven and earth system is to be governed from a city called the Holy City, New Jerusalem (Rev. 21:2). The new creation differs from the present as follows: no more sea (21:1), no more tears (21:4), no more death (21:4), and no more sorrow, crying, or pain (21:4). It should be noted that with no more sea there is still a river coming out of the throne (22:1) which runs down and out all over the earth to provide water to the trees and wherever else it is needed.

The promise of blessing and the contrast of that which is outside the city is emphatic in Revelation 21:5–8. John writes: "Then He who sat on the throne said, 'Behold I make all things new.' And He said to me, 'Write, for these words are true and faithful.' And He said to me, 'It is done! I am the Alpha and the Omega, the beginning and the end. I will give of the fountain of the water of life freely to him who thirsts. He who overcomes shall inherit all things, and I will be his God and he shall be My Son. But the cowardly, unbelieving, abominable, murderers, sexually immoral, sorcerers, idolaters, and all liars shall have their part in the lake which burns with fire and brimstone which is the second death.'" This last verse (8), along with 22:11, clearly marks this as the eternal condition, and there is now no change possible for those that passed through the previous dispensations without putting their faith in the Christ.

Revelation 21:9–22:5 delineate the physical features of the city. John writes: "Then one of the seven angels who had the seven bowls filled with the seven last plagues came to me and talked with me, saying, Come, I will show you the bride, the Lamb's wife. And he carried me away in the spirit to a great and high mountain, and showed me the great city, the holy Jerusalem, descending out of heaven from God, having the glory of God, and her light was like a most precious stone, like a jasper stone, clear as crystal" (Rev. 21:9–11). Two important points are made here. First of all, this is the city whose builder and maker is the God that all the believers of Hebrews chapter 11 have looked for from the time of Abel. Secondly, the word translated *light* in verse 11 is the Greek word *phoster*, which means a brilliant light. This place glows like the sun!

Revelation 21:12–21 describes a real city with walls, gates, dimensions, and materials. Verses 12–14 state: "Also she had a great and high wall with twelve gates, and twelve angels at the gates, and names written on them which are of the twelve tribes of the children of Israel: three gates on the east, three gates on the north, three gates on the south, and three gates on the west. Now the wall of the city had twelve foundations, and on them were the names of the twelve apostles of the Lamb." These verses show the true relation of the leaders of the faithful before Christ's advent and after. The word translated *foundations* implies that this city rests on the earth and is not suspended in the air. Verses 15–17 give some clear dimensions as John writes: "And he who talked with me had a gold reed to measure the city, its gates, and its wall. And the city is laid out as a square, and its length is as great as its breadth. And he measured the city with the reed: twelve thousand furlongs. Its length, breadth, and height are equal. Then he measured its wall: one hundred and forty-four cubits, according to the measure of a man, that is, of an angel" (apparently men and angels will be the same size in eternity as we are now). The Greek word *stadion*, which is translated *furlong* in the English is the length of a Greek Olympic stadium. The 12,000 furlongs converts to a distance of roughly 1500 statute miles. The square base from the Greek word *tetragonos* only applies to the base. This word, *tetragonos*, describes a polygon which is two dimensional (pentagons, hexagons, and octagons are all polygons) not a polyhedron, which is three dimensional. If the writer, John, was describing the whole city, i.e. anything but the base floor plan, he would not have used this word.

The wall is only 144 cubits (the length of a man's forearm and extended fingers), so the wall is only 216 feet high. Thus the statement that the height of the city is also 1500 miles probably means that the city is a *pyramid*. This makes sense when we see the river proceeding from the throne (Rev. 22:1), and the throne at the apex of the city which may be what Ezekiel saw. This would also be God's answer to the concept of man at Babel and afterward around the world that the building of pyramids/ziggurats was an object of the divine configuration in which to dwell. It also explains God's comment and judgment at Babel. Consider, if the people understood that God would build a city that was promised to look like the tower, and that He would dwell there with His people how would they respond to Nimrod building such a city. Nimrod builds this city at Babel, and puts himself in the place of God we can now understand God's statement that the people were trying to make a name for themselves and take on the aspirations to be as God (Gen. 11:1–9), which is the same thing Satan imagined as discussed in chapter 3.

The materials seen in verses 18–21 are not only seen as precious and pure, but both Philo and Josephus see in them a correspondence to the jewels on the high priest's garment. The construction of its wall was jasper, and the city was pure gold, like clear glass. The foundations of the wall of the city were adorned with all kinds of precious stones: the first foundation was jasper, the second sapphire, the third chalcedony, the fourth emerald, the fifth sardonyx, the sixth sardius, the seventh chrysolite, the eighth beryl, the ninth topaz, the tenth chrysoprase, the eleventh jacinth, and the twelfth amethyst (Rev. 21:18–20).

Revelation 22:1 sees "a pure river of living water" (a common thought in this passage, 21:6 and 22:17, as well as Jesus' word in John 4:14 and 7:38). This river is "clear as crystal, proceeding from the throne of God and of the Lamb." The oneness of God and His Son the Lamb is seen here; there is but one throne as also in 22:3, and as seen in Col. 2:9, Heb. 1:3, and 1 Cor. 15:28, a verse with eternal relationship in mind.

Revelation 22:2 sees this river, flowing down throughout the city, as being lined with trees "which bore twelve fruits, each yielding its fruit every month." There is a tie here with Ezekiel who saw the river flowing out of Jerusalem into the world with an ever-widening influence and with trees along the banks, as well as the idea of healing being provided (Ezek. 47:1–12). This implies a new calendar with eternal progression of events so we will go on in the eternal city with events and things to do as we live and reign with the Creator.

It appears from 21:24–27 that the city will be open to "the nations of those who are saved" (verse 24), and we will come and go in administering the "honoring" of God throughout the earth. The new earth thus will have a capitol, which is this "New Jerusalem" which God created for "His people" (21:2–3), from which all the earth is administered by God and His children. The new earth is apparently divided into nations (21:24) who bring their glory and honor to Jerusalem and receive the healing fruit (22:2). These nations [Gk. ethnos], that do not dwell in the city with the premillenial believers, and thus are separate from those who came from this evil world and who are promised to live and reign with Christ, are most probably the saved ones out of the millennium. This could be a vast number of people who have propagated in the millennium for 1000 years, and now inhabit the new earth.

There will be no night (verse 25), nor any sun or moon in the new system (verse 23). It is also clear that this entire scenario is based on the Genesis record as literal history since the statement is made that the curse of Genesis 3 is no more (Rev. 22:3). There is pure water in the river of life proceeding out of the throne, and trees of life, which provide twelve kinds of fruit. These trees of life, which go all the way back to Genesis chapter 3, will be reconstituted in the eternal city (Rev. 22:2). There will be no night because eternal light is provided by the Creator. Nor will we need rest, and therefore there will be no lamp or sun (Rev. 22:5). We whose names are written in the book of life (21:27) will be servants of God (22:3). It is clear that in this eternal kingdom we will have work to do in service to the Lord. Our assignments will be commensurate with our faithfulness in this life, as Jesus points out in this same revelation stating: "My reward is with me to give every man according as his work shall be" (Rev. 22:12). The Scripture goes on to say that we will see His face (22:4), and reign forever and ever (22:5).

This is the "best place" promised to all who believe (Jn. 14:1–6). Inside this beautiful city, which is 1500 miles square at the base, and 1500 miles high to the peak (21:16), are all the godly seed (Rev. 22:14). While this city is enormous, capable of housing forty billion people of our present physical size, it is not unlimited in size. This tells us that there is a limit to the size of God's family, and hence a limit to the ongoing creation of souls on this earth, and a time limit for such. In short, the seven-millennium period for this process makes some sense which is another reason to believe the Genesis time line. This thought should also spur those who believe that we are in a *race* to spread the gospel, a term which the Scripture uses repeatedly (1 Cor. 9:24; 2 Tim. 4:7; Heb. 12:1).

This eternal city is not one made with hands, but is one which came down out of heaven made by God (Jn. 14:1–3; Heb. 11:10; Rev. 21 and 22). The New Jerusalem is indeed all we could hope for and need as we live in the eternal presence of the eternal One. A miraculous hope for mankind. The real purpose of God in our creation.

CHAPTER 10

Conclusion: Battle Plan for Believers in the Last Days

In this world you shall have persecution.

—Jesus

I can only offer blood, sweat and tears.

—Churchill, 1940

Which way shall we turn to save our lives and the future of the world? . . . but I find it poignant to look at youth and wonder what would lie before them if God wearied of mankind.

—Churchill, regarding his government's decision to manufacture an H-bomb, 1955

In conclusion, we have tried to present a comprehensive overview of the scriptural, scientific, and historical record of God's plan for the ages. This monograph has been built around the classic conviction, held by philosophers from Aristotle on, and by Christian theologians from the first Christian century to today, (the apostles Paul and John, Polycarp, Patrick, Aquinas, Calvin, Schaeffer et al.) that the world is intelligible. Yes, even the events of 9–11 are intelligible. This does not say that every event is explainable in the myriad of tragedies etc. that befall this fallen planet.

So in the end, the Christian must see an overview of God's sovereignty and trust Him for the outcome (Rom. 8:28). Furthermore, the worldview which makes the world intelligible is the biblical worldview that this monograph has proclaimed.

Chapter 1 set the scene for the reason for this book at this present time, reviewing the event that defines our time, i.e. 9–11.

Chapter 2 presented the case for the Genesis record as being literal, historical truth, evidenced to by scientific facts, and the foundation for an intelligible understanding of the rest of the Bible, the existence of evil, and a need for a savior. It also gives an explanation for the geologic record, and the existence of the varied ethnic groups in the world. The basic arguments for the inspired revelation called the Bible as truly the word from our Creator are also presented.

Chapter 3 presented the nature of the Creator and His purpose for mankind.

Chapter 4 is fundamental to this book's premise, that 9–11 is just the latest manifestation of *the long war against God*. This chapter explains Satan and the existence of evil, the fall of mankind, the war declared by God in Genesis 3:15, and the present status of the world and mankind under the curse.

Chapters 5 and 6 gave a brief run through 6000 years of world history and a biblical timeline. These chapter presented both scientific and historical data that should lead the reader to an understanding of what in the world God is doing. It is a narrow view of history that centers on *the long war against God* and the Seed of Satan against the Seed of God as predicted in Genesis 3:15. We are in this war!

Chapter 7 presents a scientific look at the near future, i.e. the next fifteen years, with some conclusion about the certainty of such prognostications. It also shows that we are not going to solve our problems scientifically or politically with the clash of world civilizations dominating the last days.

Chapter 8 delves into the biblical prophecy of the end times and tries to relate it to current scenarios throughout the world.

Chapter 9 has presented the biblically assured conclusion to this present age and the promise of the world to come.

Now this chapter has some thoughts of what to do in light of all this. I have characterized it as a *Battle Plan for believers: a Balanced Approach.* Mankind needs to understand the truth of Genesis, the reality of *the long war against God* and that we are soldiers in it. What then should we do? In the face of the loss of morality and orthodoxy in the Western "Christian" civilizations, the late Frances Schaeffer wrote extensively on the topic expressed by the question *How Should We Then Live?*[58] Later, Charles Colson wrote a book with essentially the same title. We have now entered into an entirely different world with the events of September 11. Now, in the face of this current crisis, we ask ourselves the same question. Well, it is not all that difficult to figure out, if we take some fundamental guidelines from the Word of God. With the following in mind, the specific acts of servanthood will not be difficult to decide.

1. Study and Witness

As stated in the introduction, this monograph represents a worldview based on transcendent truths as revealed in the Word of God. This is a rational approach to a world in chaos, rather than an irrational view based on personal experience, charismatic wonders, or temporal expedience. Furthermore, our worldview is based on the Genesis record, rational science, and not the lie of evolution. As such, it is our challenge to continually search the Scriptures just as the apostles Peter (1 Pet. 1:10–12) and Paul (2 Tim. 3:16–17) said, and study so that we may be fully equipped to understand and face the present danger.

A unique door of opportunity is open to us: this is a unique time in the nation of Israel and many Jews are already recognizing that Jesus (Yeshua) is the Messiah (HaMashiach). So witness and pray for the peace of Jerusalem!

This is also a unique time in the lives of our enemies. Pray that they will hear the truth and be saved before it is too late for them. Everybody we speak to will want to talk about the events of these last days. Until the tactic that we are employing to defeat terrorism and divide Islam and other evil rulers from their subjects is rejected, there will be a window of opportunity to reach out to the people under Islam's control. According to *Understanding and Responding to Islam* by Dr. Patrick Cate, the data shows that seventy-seven percent of the Arabs in the USA have already put their trust in Christ and rejected Islam. Islam teaches that if you die in Holy War (Jihad) while killing thousands you will go to paradise. Christianity marks the day that God sent His Son to live and die for mankind, paying the penalty for Adam's and therefore every man's sins. All mankind lies in Adam and so all mankind dies as Genesis and the apostle Paul declares (Rom. 5:12). God has redeemed this Satan-induced situation through Jesus, the second Adam (Rom. 5:15–21) that everyone who believes Him will not die but live forever in paradise with Him. Furthermore, what God did in giving His Son was done in love (Jn. 3:16); our dealing with the lost and satanically deluded enemies of Christ must also be done in love, for God in Christ told us to love our enemies (Matt. 5:43, 44). What a marked difference between Christianity and Islam!

2. Fight!

While some may advocate pacifism as the truly Christian approach to these last days, we need to understand what God has really told His people to do in the face of evil. While Jesus does teach that we are to turn the other cheek and love our enemies on an individual basis, nowhere did He speak out against the use of military force as a function of government to stop murderers or thieves. Paul, in his letter to the church at Rome, gives the proper balance as he writes, "Pay back to no man evil for evil . . . avenge not yourselves . . . overcome evil with good" (Rom. 12:17–21). This passage is immediately followed with the responsibility of the believers who are to be subject to just governmental rulers which are to be "a terror to evil . . . for he (this ruler) is a minister of God, an avenger to execute wrath upon him that doeth evil" (Rom. 13:1–4).

As images of God we are responsible to challenge evil and stop it with all our might. We are charged to proclaim the truth! (Matt. 28:19–20). Fight for the truth of the gospel (1 Tim. 6:12), which states that all other ways to eternal life apart from faith in Christ are false and will be condemned (Rev. 20:15). Support our government as long as our president is a believer (Note what the apostle Peter told the unbelieving rulers of his day, when he was told to desist declaring that Jesus was the only way Acts 4:19), and a terror to evil (Rom. 13). This terror to evil in the form of government should wield the sword (Rom. 13:4) which means life for life, and justifies war and death penalties for those who take life unjustly.

God has always had His warriors in this fight as we study the lives of Joshua, Caleb, various judges, prophets, and kings of His people such as David. There is an explosion of evil in these last days. We ask, "What is the world coming to?" It is coming to the Day of Judgment! Vengeance belongs to Jesus who with His army is coming to destroy this evil, just as He said (Matt. 24:30–31). Revelation 19 depicts Him as coming as King of kings and Lord of lords and He "treads the winepress of the fierceness and wrath of Almighty God" (Rev. 19:15). Jesus does not delight in the death of the wicked, as He is both a caring savior and a just God. David wrote, "Kiss the Son, lest He be angry, and ye perish" (Ps. 2:12). Paul wrote that Jesus and His mighty angels will take "vengeance on them that know not God, and obey not the gospel of our Lord Jesus Christ" (2 Thess. 1:8). Jesus, in discussing these days, said to those who do not believe in Him, "Depart from Me, ye, cursed, into everlasting fire" (Matt. 25:41).

The long war against God which was started in the Garden of Eden by Satan is ongoing today between the forces of evil and the forces for good. The highest good is not earthly peace, but heavenly peace, which will not be brought in until the Prince of Peace (Isa. 9:6), the Lord Jesus, returns to live and reign on earth. We who are in the body of Christ, set for the kingdom to come, are God's warriors today. Onward Christian soldiers!

3. Pray in These last days!

The singular most prominent task that Jesus taught us to do, both by example and precept, is to pray. The prevailing highly visible existence of evil in these last days can be a reason for faint hearts to just quit. Many in the nation of Israel have come to this point. We might ask what real hope do we have that we can prevent evil, or wage war, and be triumphant in the struggle of this age. It should be understood that nothing can occur without passing through God's filter (Rom. 8:28 etc.). Jesus told us that we have power to do something about the evil of this present age and how to access that power. In His confrontation with Peter, Jesus said that He had prayed that Satan would not have dominion over Peter and that Peter's "faith would not fail" (Lk. 22:32). The prayer that Jesus taught His disciples to pray, and henceforth all His disciples to pray, was a clear asking of God to "deliver us from the evil one" (Lk. 11:4). The Greek word used here is properly translated *evil one* just as the Scripture gives us the same word in John 17:15. Jesus very clearly prays here for us to remain in this world and be kept from the evil one.

Thus, prayer is the path to defeat the evil in this present age. This prayer should be a daily occurrence as the petition for daily bread is included in the prayer. It should be understood that prayer is a real and effectual stand against the presence of evil in the world. It is our foremost weapon. Therefore, as the children of God we must pray, for we are at war! We know that "we wrestle not against flesh and blood, but against principalities, against powers, against the rulers of the darkness of this world, against spiritual wickedness in high places" (Eph. 6:12). The battleground is prayer (Eph. 6:18). In should be noted that when the prophet Daniel prayed, as recorded in Daniel chapter ten, it took twenty-one days for God's angels to overcome the evil angel, the prince of the kingdom of Persia. It is obvious that we, like Daniel, are included in this battle. We who believe in Jesus, the Son of God, who is coming to live and reign on Earth, are all soldiers in a mighty army, each one with a unique role in this time. The apostle Peter said that, "we are begotten to a living hope . . . reserved in heaven . . . kept to the last time . . . now for a season in manifold trials" (1 Pet. 1:3–7), and when "the end of all things is at hand; be sober minded and watch unto prayer" (1 Pet. 4:7). NOW is the time!

We have heavenly angels on our side waiting for our directive prayers, as was seen in Daniel chapter ten. Pray for our nation's leaders that they may know the path God would have for them as they deal with the present evil. Pray for protection for our families, friends, and fighting men that God would protect them from the evil one (Lk. 11:4). Pray when you get up in the morning, when you lie down at night, and without ceasing.

Conclusion

It is believed that this monograph has defined for the reader the fundamental purpose of the universe in a unique correlation of the biblical record, the secular historical record, and the scientific evidence. We have seen that 9–11, the true nature of anti-Semitism and evil, really do go *back* to *Genesis*. It should be understood that this *long war against God* has been going on from the time of the fall of Adam and Eve to this very day as the godly seed and the seed of Satan battle it out. We have, it could be said, tried to give a thesis of what could be called *The Theology of Everything: The Origin and Fate of the Universe*, if we can steal a concept from Stephen Hawking. Hawking wrote in his book titled *The Theory of Everything*: "If we do discover a complete theory, it should in time be understandable in broad principle to everyone, not just a few scientists. Then we shall be able to take part in the discussion of why the universe exists. If we find the answer to that, it would be the ultimate triumph of human reason. For then we would know the mind of God." I believe this monograph, which began in Genesis and ends in Revelation, reveals the mind of God, why the universe exists, and His plan for mankind in this age and the age to come.

The biblical worldview of war, despair, pain, and suffering has been characterized by the atheist Sigmund Freud as "certainly not anything one would wish for."[59] We truly do not wish for war, but rather for peace, but we must not compromise truth for peace nor accommodate the evil nations to achieve a temporary peace. The biblical worldview from Genesis to Revelation affirms the Creation and the Fall, a satanically influenced era where War is ordained. God reveals His solution to the fall and plans for this age and the ages to come. It affirms the objectivity of moral truth, and the existence of a transcendent Creator God who became incarnate, who died, and rose from death, purchasing eternal life for all who believe (Jn. 3:16–19).

Middle East scholar and Institute for Peace director Daniel Pipes has pointed out terrorism's militant Islamic roots. He has tried to say that a moderate Islam is the solution. It is clearly stated in Islamic law that no people may rule territory once possessed by Muslims. Palestine and Jerusalem were conquered by Muslims in A.D. 641. Furthermore, Islam has said that Muslims may not be ruled over by non-Muslims *anywhere!* Therefore, there will be no peace in Israel until the world rulers enforce it, probably under the antichrist, and then it will be short lived. The truth is, we will not stop war in this age! Christ is the solution to the edict of Genesis 3:15, and there will be no true peace until the Prince of Peace (Isa. 9:6) returns to enforce it. What we can expect in the near future was spelled out by Christ, and we are soon to enter into a period of tribulation such as the world has never seen (Matt. 24:21, 22). With regard to tribulation Jesus said "In the world you will have tribulation; but be of good cheer, I have overcome the world!" (Jn. 16:33). What He meant by that statement is His ability by His completed work at Calvary to deliver us beyond this time era into the Sabbath rest of the millennial kingdom, to be followed by that city that all true believers look for (Heb. 11:10) which truly is the best place, as spelled out in the previous chapter. It is as sure as the book of Genesis is literal, historical, truth.

End Notes

1. The Friends of Israel is a Hebrew/Christian ministry located in Bellmar, NJ that seeks to bring the truth about Jesus the Messiah to the Jews and an unbelieving world.

2. Morris, H. M., *The Genesis Record*, 1993, Baker Book House, Grand Rapids, MI, p. 17.

3. Fred Hoyle and Chandra Wicramasinghe, *Evolution in Space*, 1982, Simon & Schuster, NY.

4. Fred Hoyle and Chandra Wicramasinghe, "Where Microbes Boldly Went" *New Scientist.* 91, 1981, pp. 412–415.

5. Nicholi, Armand, *The Question of God*, 2003, Free Press, New York, NY, p. 45.

6. McConkie, Bruce, *Mormon Doctrine*, 1966, Bookcraft, SLC, UT. p. 257 Doctrine of Exaltation.

7. Morris, H.M., *The Long War Against God*, 1990, Baker Book House, Grand Rapids, MI.

8. Barnes, T.G. *Origin and Destiny of the Earth's Magnetic Field*, 1873. ICR, El Cahon, CA.

9. Davey, K.R. "Eigenvalue Analysis of the Magnetic Field of the Earth and its Implications on Age and Field Reversal," proceedings of Second International Conference on Creationism Vol. II, Technical Sessions, 1990, CSF, Pittsburgh PA.

10. Ussher, James, *The Annals of the World*, 2003, Master Books, Green Forest, AR, This work was originally published in Latin in 1658 by Oliver Cromwell, and contains over 10,000 references of world history from the earliest writing to A.D. 70.

11. Curtis, W. M., *The Forgotten Feast*, 1985, Brentwood Christian Press, Columbus, GA.

12. Martin, E.L., "The Celestial Pageantry Dating Christ's Birth" *Christianity Today*.

13. Wang, Kuzmich, and Dogariu, "Speed of Light," *Nature*, 7/20/2000.

14. Coles, P. and Lucchin, F., *Cosmology: The Origin and Evolution of Cosmic Structures*, 1996, John Wiley & Sons Ltd. Chichester, UK.

15. Mageuijo, Joao, *Faster Than the Speed of Light*, 2003, Perseus Publishing, Cambridge, MA. Dr. Magueijo is a professor of theoretical physics at Imperial College in London.

16. Filkin, David, *Stephen Hawking's Universe*, 1997, BasicBooks/Harper Collins, New York, NY.

17. Proceedings of the Second International Conference on Creationism, 2 vol., 1990, CSF Pittsburgh, PA.

18. Proceedings of the Fourth International Conference on Creationism, 1998, CSF Pittsburgh, PA.

19. Proceedings of the Fifth International Conference on Creationism 2003, CSF Pittsburgh, PA.

20. Livingston, David, *Search for Noah's Ark*, ISBR Forum, 2-6-03, Lancaster, PA.

21. ICR Impact paper #366, Dec. 2003, ICR, El Cajon, CA.

22. Gish, Duane T., *Evolution: the fossils still say No!*, 1995, Inst. for Creation Research, El Cajon, CA, p. 57.

23. Dawkins, Richard, *The Blind Watchmaker*, 1987, W.W. Norton, NY, p. 229.

24. Sarfatti, Jonathan, "DNA: marvelous messages," *Creation*, Vol. 25-2, Mar-May 2003, AIG Australia, Acacia Ridge DC, Qld 4110 and Weiland, C. "Sensational Dinosaur Blood Report!" *Creation*, Vol. 19 (4): 42-43, Sept.-Nov. 1997, or www.answersingenesis.org.

25. Whitcomb, John and Morris, Henry, *The Genesis Flood*, 1961, Presbyterian and Reformed Pub., Phillipsburg, NJ.

26. Broadbent, E.H., *The Pilgrim Church*, 1999, Gospel Folio Press, Grand Rapids, MI.

27. Curtis, W.M., *Specific Revelation*, 1993, Brentwood Christian Press, Columbus, GA.

28. Bullinger, E.W. *Witness of the Stars*, 1967, Kregel, Grand Rapids, MI.

29. Pentecost, Dwight, *Things to Come*, 1960, Dallas Seminary Press, Dallas, TX.

30. Harris, Archer, and Waltke, *Theological Wordbook of the Old Testament*, 1980, Moody Press, Chicago, IL.

31. Plato, *Timaeus*, 1977, 12 volumes, Harvard University Press, Cambridge, MA.

32. *Atlantis and the Days of Peleg*, a paper presented by Dr. W. M. Curtis at the Lancaster creation forum Dec. 2001. Video available from The Institute for Scientific and Biblical Research, 128 Round Hill Lane, Lancaster, PA 17603.

33. "Destruction of Christianity in Japan" *World Magazine*, Aug. 2003, Asheville, NC.

34. Yasutani, Hakum, *Zen Buddhism*, 1943, Published in Japan during WW II.

35. McCullough, David, *John Adams*, 2001, Simon & Schuster, New York, NY.

36. McCullough, David, *John Adams*, 2001, Simon & Schuster, New York, NY, p. 418.

37. Morey, Robert, *The Islamic Invasion*, 1997, Christian Scholars Press.

38. Gold, Dore, *Hatred's Kingdom*, 2003, Regnery Publishing, Washington, D.C.

39. Huntington, Samuel P., *The Clash of Civilizations and the Remaking of World Order*, 1996, Touchstone/Simon & Schuster, New York, NY.

40. Lam, Nora, *China Cry*, 1990, and *The Battle for the Chinese Bible*, 1997, Nora Lam Chinese Ministries International, San Jose, CA.

41. Monteith, Stanley, *Brotherhood of Darkness*, 2000, Hearthstone Publishing, Oklahoma City, OK.

42. Gore, Al, *The Earth in the Balance*, 1993, Penguin Books, New York, NY.

43. Ehrlich, Paul, *The Population Bomb*, 1968, Buccaneer Books, Cutchogue, NY.

44. "Population Implosion" *World Magazine*, Feb. 15, 2003.

45. *2015 Global Trends*, 2000, U.S. Government Printing Office Stock #041-015-00211-2.

46. Beck, Paul, "Cleaning up Old King Coal," *Popular Science*, May 2002.

47. "The Kyoto Protocol and Global Warming" *Imprimis*, March 2002, Hillsdale College, MI.

48. Paul Kurtz, ed. *The Humanist Manifesto I and II*, 1973, Prometheus Books, Buffalo, NY, p. 16.

49. Tanner, Jerald & Sandra., *Mormonism Shadow or Reality*, 1987, Utah Lighthouse Ministries, Salt Lake City, UT.

50. "The Red Heifer," *Israel My Glory*, May 2002, Friends of Israel, Bellmar, NJ.

51. Showers, Renald E., *What on Earth is God Doing?*, 1973, Loizeaux Brothers, Neptune, NJ.

52. Showers, Renald E., *Those Invisible Spirits Called Angels*, 1997, The Friends of Israel Gospel Ministry, Bellmawr, NJ.

53. *Encyclopedia Judaica*, 11 Vol., 1971. Macmillan, New York.

54. Congdon, Robert, "The European Union" tapes available from Friends of Israel, Bellmar, NJ, Fall 2003 Conference at Willow Valley, PA.

55. Burleigh, Michael, *The Third Reich*, 2000, Hill & Wang, New York, NY.

56. Babylonian Talmud: Sanhedrin 97b.

57. Curtis, W. M. *Specific Revelation*, 1993, Brentwood Christian Press, Columbus, GA.

58. Schaeffer, Francis A., *How Should We Then Live?*, 1976, Fleming Revell, Old Tappan, NJ.

59. Nicholi, Armand, *The Question of God*, 2003, Free Press, New York, NY.

60. Gade, Richard, *A Historical View of Antisemitism,* 1981, Baker Book House, Grand Rapids, MI.

61. Marshall, Paul, *Their Blood Cries Out,* 1997 Word Publishing, Dallas, TX.

62. Frankl, Viktor, *The Doctor and the Soul: Introduction to Logotherapy,* 1982, NY: Knopf, xxi.

63. Sarfatti, Jonathan, *Refuting Compromise*, 2004, Master Books, Green Forest, AR.

Index

To order additional copies of

The Last Days
of the
Longest War

Have your credit card ready and call

Toll free: (877) 421-READ (7323)

or send $13.99* each plus $4.95 S&H** to

WinePress Publishing
PO Box 428
Enumclaw, WA 98022

or order online at: www.winepresspub.com

*WA residents, add 8.4% sales tax

**add $1.50 S&H for each additional book ordered